LIBRARY OF CONGRESS

Motion Pictures, Broadcasting, Recorded Sound

AN ILLUSTRATED GUIDE

LIBRARY OF CONGRESS   WASHINGTON   2002

This publication was made possible by generous support from the James Madison Council, a national, private-sector advisory council dedicated to helping the Library of Congress share its unique resources with the nation and the world.

Motion Pictures, Broadcasting, Recorded Sound is composed in Centaur, a typeface designed by American Typography and book designer Bruce Rogers (1870–1957). The full type font was first used at the Montague Press in 1915 for an edition of Maurice de Guérin's *The Centaur.*

This guide was written by Alan Gevinson, Joan Higbee, and staff of the Motion Picture, Broadcasting, and Recorded Sound Division, under the direction of Samuel Brylawski. It was edited by Iris Newsom, Publishing Office, designed by Robert L. Wiser, Archetype Press, Inc., Washington, D.C., and directed by Gloria Baskerville-Holmes, Production Manager, Publishing Office.

COVER: Nanook, played by Allakariallak, being introduced to the joys of recorded sound. Detail from *Nanook of the North*, 1922.

LIBRARY OF CONGRESS CATALOGING-IN-PUBLICATION DATA

Library of Congress. Motion Picture, Broadcasting, and Recorded Sound Division.
    Library of Congress motion pictures, broadcasting, recorded sound : an illustrated guide.
       p.   cm.
    ISBN 0-8444-0988-X
    1. Library of Congress. Motion Picture, Broadcasting, and Recorded Sound Division. 2. Motion pictures — Washington (D.C.) — Library resources. 3. Broadcasting — Washington (D.C.) — Library resources. 4. Sound recordings — Washington (D.C.) — Library resources.
    PN1993.4.L53 2001
    [Z663.36]
    026'.7914'09753 — dc21
                                          00 — 050019

For sale by the Superintendent of Documents, U.S. Government Printing Office
Internet: bookstore.gpo.gov   Phone: (202) 512-1800   Fax: (202) 512-2250
Mail: Stop SSOP, Washington, DC 20402-0001

ISBN 0-16-050932-7

Contents

Introduction

THE RICH COLLECTIONS of the Library of Congress Motion Picture, Broadcasting, and Recorded Sound Division (MBRS) document the past one hundred years, the audiovisual century, the first century to be recorded by sound and moving images. We will never know the sound of Abraham Lincoln's voice at Gettysburg or hear Beethoven playing the piano, but library and archival collections today are abundant with the sights and sounds of the century. Through radio and television broadcasts and newsreels, the young of today can experience nearly firsthand the charisma of John F. Kennedy, the persuasiveness of Franklin D. Roosevelt, the spectacle of Adolf Hitler, and the artistry of Louis Armstrong. The collections of the Motion Picture, Broadcasting, and Recorded Sound Division offer abundant testimony to the media experiences that swayed our contemporaries as well as their parents and grandparents: not only the news broadcasts and documentary films, but the popular music, grand opera, soap operas, poetry, lyric drama, docudrama, and quiz shows too. Thanks to recorded sound and moving images, our times will be better known and understood than preceding centuries.

With the privilege of holding the significant cultural and historical audiovisual documents of the past century comes the responsibility of maintaining that archive for centuries to come. However, while motion pictures, broadcasting tapes, and sound recordings are ubiquitous and available to nearly everyone when new, these documents are among the most fragile held by archives, and among the most difficult for libraries to preserve and maintain. For that reason, the Motion Picture, Broadcasting, and Recorded Sound Division is establishing the National Audio-Visual Conservation Center (NAVCC), a forty-one acre campus in Culpeper, Virginia, dedicated to the preservation of our audiovisual heritage. The Center was established by extraordinary gifts from the David and Lucile Packard Foundation and the Packard Humanities Institute. The Center will comprise custom-designed cold temperature and humidity-controlled vaults for tapes, films, and sound recordings and two preservation laboratories for the reformatting of fragile audiovisual materials to the most stable analog and digital media available.

One hundred years ago, in the closing years of the nineteenth century, Washington, D.C., was at the center of the nascent motion picture and sound recording industries. The commercial and creative centers of those businesses soon passed to other cities. With the new century upon us, Washington is again a media center. It is not only a region in which many important Internet-related businesses are based and an important news center, it is the home of what will be the foremost repository and conservation facility for our audiovisual history. The

OPPOSITE. *The Absent-Minded Professor* (Walt Disney Productions, 1961; distributed by Buena Vista Distribution Company). Fred MacMurray and Nancy Olson fly high over the U.S. Capitol and the Library of Congress. *(Copyright © 1961 Walt Disney Company)*

NAVCC will ensure that the sound and moving image documents which record our history and shape people's views of our times will be available for study and pleasure for many centuries to come. This brief guide to our collections will provide readers with a description of some of the activities of, and treasures in the Motion Picture, Broadcasting, and Recorded Sound Division—including those destined to be housed in the vaults at Culpeper in the next few years—and it also describes the preservation responsibilities inherent in caring for these riches.

DAVID J. FRANCIS, CHIEF
MOTION PICTURE, BROADCASTING, AND RECORDED SOUND DIVISION

RIGHT. In 1889, the Columbia Phonograph Company was established in the heart of the nation's capital. By 1891, a government publication reported, "More phonographs are in practical use in Washington than in any other city in the country, not excepting New York." The phonograph failed as a dictation machine, its originally intended commercial use, but succeeded as a music medium, first in phonograph parlors, later for the home. Columbia recorded many of the early phonograph's most popular artists, such as the U.S. Marine Band and John Philip Sousa's band, in this building, which is still standing in downtown Washington, D.C.

OPPOSITE. The National Audio-Visual Conservation Center at Culpeper, Virginia, will provide the best care possible for the nation's audiovisual riches. The Center's building for the storage of the collections of the Motion Picture, Broadcasting, and Recorded Sound Division is built into the side of a small mountain. Such construction helps to assure that temperature and humidity levels in the vaults will remain constant.

BEGINNING IN THE LATE 1880s, Washington, D.C., was established by inventors and businessmen as the national center for recording and disseminating motion pictures and sound recordings. The work of the Volta Laboratory resuscitated the dormant talking machine industry and forced Edison, who had abandoned the phonograph to develop the lightbulb, to develop further the talking machine. The local franchise that was created to exploit the Phonograph that had been improved by the inventions of Bell and Edison was called the Columbia Phonograph Company, after the District of Columbia.

Around the same time, about one mile east of the Volta Laboratory, a young German inventor, Emile Berliner, was independently developing a new type of talking machine, a flat disc recording and playback system he called the Gramophone. After working for several years in the nascent telephone industry, during which time he invented a loose contact transmitter that would eventually become the first radio microphone, Berliner turned his attention to the science of recording and reproducing sound. By 1887, his experimentation resulted in a patented method for laterally tracing sound vibrations onto a fatty-substance-coated zinc disc and etching them into the zinc with an acid bath, thereby fixing the grooves permanently onto the disc. In addition, Berliner experimented with record compounds, ultimately settling on shellac for its hardness, indestructibility, and ability to produce a loud, crisp sound. Because shellac could be molded, his methods enabled the manufacture of virtually limitless numbers of pressings from master recordings. Cylinder recordings at that time could not be molded and mass produced. In 1986, Berliner teamed with machinist Eldridge R. Johnson to make further improvements to the Gramophone. After litigation forced Berliner to close down his American operations in 1900, their company evolved into the Victor Talking Machine Company, under the direction of Johnson. Berliner associate and fellow-Washingtonian Fred Gaisberg was the record industry's first "producer." In addition to providing piano accompaniment and overseeing recording in nineteenth-century Washington, D.C., Gaisberg made many recording expeditions to Europe, Asia, and the Far East. It was Gaisberg who signed up tenor Enrico Caruso for his first recording contract, which he did against the wishes of his employer, who believed Caruso was demanding too much money.

Through the generosity and cooperation of Mr. Berliner's descendants, particularly his grandson Robert Sanders, the Library of Congress possesses over five hundred published and unpublished Berliner discs as well as laboratory notebooks, personal scrapbooks, business and legal papers, and materials relating

ABOVE. Fred Gaisberg termed Leonid Sobinov the greatest lyric tenor in Russia and recorded him in Moscow in 1901. This Sobinov recording, Verdi's "La donna e mobile" (sung in Russian) is one of hundreds of rare acoustic recordings made in Russia that are included in the Joel Berger Collection at the Library.

OPPOSITE. The Motion Picture, Broadcasting, and Recorded Sound (MBRS) collections include an array of rare books on audiovisual topics, including *Animated Pictures* (1898) by visionary inventor C. Francis Jenkins. Shown here is a Phonograph parlor featuring Jenkins's Phantoscope, a coin-in-the-slot motion picture machine.

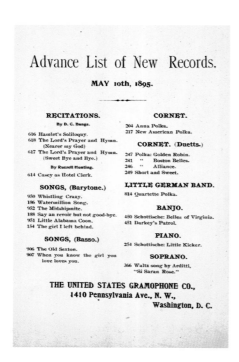

The content of the Berliner recordings reflects the standard repertory of the time: popular music, traditional songs, funny stories, band performances, instrumental solos, whistling, and recitations. Of particular interest are what could be the first recordings of Native American chants, various local Washington performers, John Philip Sousa's band, and some of the earliest recordings of opera.

to his extensive philanthropic work in Washington. With the Berliner family's support, the Library has become the largest single source of information on the life and work of this important inventor.

Washington, D.C., media developments were not limited to the Phonograph and Gramophone. The first successful attempts at broadcasting sound by radio would follow early in the new century. C. Francis Jenkins published an article detailing an idea for the electronic transmission of pictures in July 1894. In 1923, he gave the first laboratory demonstration of his invention, which he called "Radio Vision" and was later to be renamed "television." A proud Washington resident, Jenkins delivered a talk on a 1924 radio broadcast entitled "Washington, the City of Enchantment," in which he called his adopted home "the scientific center of the world."

Jenkins had earlier invented the first motion picture projector with another Washingtonian, Thomas Armat. He also developed a coin-in-the-slot motion picture viewer, the Phantascope, which was exhibited in the Pure Foods Exposition in Washington, D.C., in November 1894. The Phantoscope had an effect on Edison's development of the motion picture similar to that of Bell on Edison's talking machine: Armat's and Jenkins's innovations considerably improved the projection of motion pictures, and projectors combining the patents of each were soon marketed successfully. The fruits of these inventions made it possible to create the Library of Congress's first audiovisual collection from paper prints.

As a result of the 1865 amendment to the United States' copyright law and the subsequent copyright act of 1870, the Library of Congress became the national repository of materials deposited for copyright protection. The scope of creations which could be copyrighted included books, pamphlets, maps, charts, musical compositions, prints, engravings, and photographs. Owners of motion pictures who wished to be protected from illegal duplication printed each frame of their films onto paper stock and submitted the paper rolls as photographs to be copyrighted. Though part of the Library's collection, their historic value was not recognized for nearly fifty years because they could not be projected as film prints.

In his Annual Report for fiscal year 1942, Librarian of Congress Archibald MacLeish reported the following matter: "An examination of ancient copyright deposits in the Library cellars has brought to light an extraordinary collection … of rolls of prints of the earliest moving pictures exposed on paper as photographs." The next year, he announced the beginning of a project "to restore, organize, and administer a collection of motion pictures." The extreme brittleness of the old paper rolls—many of which had become twisted and cracked and were impossible to

RIGHT. Alexander Graham Bell's Washington, D.C., Volta Laboratory improved upon Thomas Edison's 1877 invention, the tinfoil phonograph. Volta Laboratory engineers Charles Sumner Tainter and Chichester A. Bell created the first practical sound recording system, called the Graphophone. Phonograph was a trade name owned by Edison. The Graphophone's improvements over the phonograph included its wax coating and modulation recorded in grooves by engraving rather than embossing.

LEFT. Bubble Books were a popular twentieth-century children's book series of the teens. Each Bubble Book included small 78 rpm discs of songs that were to be played as the stories were read. Bubble Books were the first sound recordings regularly received by the Library of Congress. Children's books on cassettes remain a very popular format.

Copyright registration form for *The Un-veiling of the Washington Monument* (Lubin, 1897). The event documented in this early motion picture "actuality" took place at Fairmount Park, Philadelphia, and was attended by Pres. William McKinley and his cabinet. In the early years of motion pictures, some copyright claimants attached stills from their films to registration forms. The deterioration of nitrate film has provided film conservators with one of their most urgent challenges: to preserve as much of this quickly disappearing visual evidence of the past as possible.

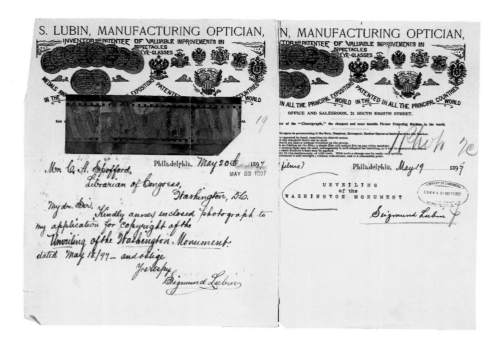

Sample photograph frame from the 1898 Mutoscope film *Pope Leo XIII in Carriage* (American Mutoscope Company). During the first several years of the American motion picture industry, before movies were regulary projected before large audiences, the leading mode of public exhibition was through "peep show" machines. The Mutoscope was the main American competitor to Edison's peep show machine, the Kinetoscope. The Mutoscope was based on the physiological principle of the "persistence of vision" and employed photographs printed in sequence from a motion picture film negative to produce the illusion of full motion. Contemporary commentators appreciated the historic significance of the new moving image medium. The *New York Mail and Express* in 1897 noted on the occasion of a screening of Biograph films, "What the invention of the alphabet has done in the preservation of the facts of history, the Biograph and kindred inventions promise to do in the restoration of historical atmosphere."

project—posed numerous difficulties for technicians attempting to copy them to safety film. In the early 1950s, in conjunction with the Academy of Motion Picture Arts and Sciences, a rephotographing technique was perfected, and appropriations by Congress made it possible to bring the rephotographing project to a successful conclusion in 1964. Today, the Paper Print Collection constitutes the world's largest and most comprehensive source of American movies from the early silent era.

Almost three hundred hours of moving image history from the dawn of American cinema—3,003 long-lost comic, dramatic, and actuality movies—have been recovered. In addition to being a rich historical record of turn-of-the-century American life, the Paper Print Collection documents the important transition period when the motion picture industry began to produce narrative comic and dramatic entertainment films. Surviving as they do in no other collection are virtually all the earliest films of Edwin S. Porter, who directed *The Great Train Robbery* (Edison, 1903), and D. W. Griffith, whose Biograph melodramas beginning in 1908 proved to be vital testing grounds for the development of expressive storytelling techniques.

Following a change in copyright law in 1912, films were finally allowed to be copyrighted as motion pictures, rather than as photographs. Depositing motion pictures at the Library, though, created a dangerous storage problem, as early nitrate film stock was highly inflammable. After 1915, when the last complete paper prints were received, the Library ceased collecting copies of motion pictures through copyright deposit, until 1942 when Archibald MacLeish reinstituted the practice, laying the foundation for the Library's unequalled motion picture collections.

Frankenstein (1910); *Primitive Man* (1913). Monsters have provided an ongoing source of fear and fascination for movie fans throughout the audiovisual century. The earliest film version of *Frankenstein* (1910), left, only survives in the paper print fragments submitted as copyright registrations to the Library. In *Primitive Man* (1913), right, also a paper print, D. W. Griffith created an ancestor to the many cinematic dinosaurs that have continued to haunt movie screens and fans' imaginations.

Formative Years

THE THIRTY YEARS between the mid-1890s and the mid-1920s witnessed the acoustical period of sound recordings, the silent era of motion pictures, prenetwork radio broadcasting, and the first inklings of experimental television. This was a period of rapid growth and false starts, of patent litigation and corporate struggles for control and expansion, and of concerted efforts to promote technical and commercial stability. During this transitional period, the power of media entertainment began to be felt in many ways. The enormous appeal to the public of media stars became a lasting legacy of these early days.

Established sites of nineteenth-century popular entertainment, such as the vaudeville stage and the opera, supplied the earliest talent to the budding companies producing moving pictures and recordings. The Paper Print Collection provides visual glimpses of some of these long-forgotten acts, such as *Marceline, the World-Renowned Clown of the New York Hippodrome; Sandow the Strongman, Miss Lillian Shaffer and Her Dancing Horse*, and *Spike, the Bag-Punching Dog*. These films allow us to experience turn-of-the-century popular performances as they appeared to audiences of the time.

While the paper print voices are silent, a multitude of sounds of the nineteenth century — elixir salesmen's pitches, stories told in dialect, vaudeville jokes, poem and prose recitations, minstrel songs, band concerts, and solo performances — have survived on records, thanks to the collections accumulated by dedicated aficionados, those who write about recordings, and other diligent collectors. The Library has some of the finest collections of disc recordings from the early acoustical period. Foremost among these are the collections of Ulysses ("Jim") Walsh, James Martindale, and George Moss, whose recordings leave to posterity the sounds of an earlier generation's popular culture.

The Walsh Collection numbers some forty thousand discs and five hundred cylinders, including an extensive run of Edison "Diamond Disc" recordings covering the years between 1912 and 1929. Voluminous printed materials donated by Walsh include rare record catalogs dating back to 1892 that provide researchers with the basic tools necessary to determine just what was recorded during the acoustic period.

Besides presenting entertainment, films and recordings from these early years documented famous people, places, and events. Motion pictures in the Library record such personages as William Jennings Bryan, presidents William McKinley and Theodore Roosevelt, Prince Henry of Prussia, Kings Edward VII and George V of England, Pres. Porfirio Díaz of Mexico, Adm. Thomas Dewey, and Sen. Mark Hanna. Early films documented places near and far, from the many

OPPOSITE. Humorist Cal Stewart, called in his time the "emperor of rural comedians," began in the 1890s to record his impersonation of "Uncle Josh Weathersby," leading citizen of the mythical New England village of "Pumpkin Center." His rollicking laugh and drawling speech made him a favorite to millions. Stewart, friend to both Mark Twain and Will Rogers, offered gems of homespun philosophy in his stories, such as the following saying of Uncle Josh: "Advice is something the other fellow can't use, so he gives it to you." Stewart recorded for all the leading companies until his death in 1919. The Library has acquired, primarily from "Jim" Walsh, several hundred recordings of Cal Stewart's performances. Still from "Cal Stewart the Yankee Story Teller," *Phonoscope* (February 1899, vol. 3, no. 2, p. 6).

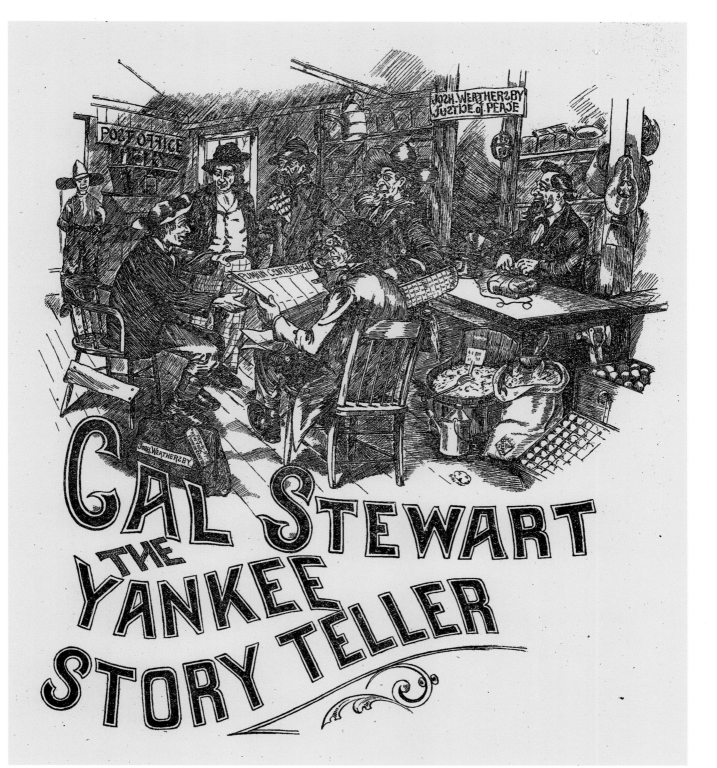

In the films of the Theodore Roosevelt Collection, the president (pictured here in a newsreel) can be seen attending McKinley's funeral in 1901, parading through the streets of San Francisco in 1903, taking the oath of office during his 1905 inaugural ceremony, and visiting Panama in November 1906—the first trip to a foreign country by an incumbent American president. Following his presidency, Roosevelt appeared in films shot during a hunting trip in Africa, the funeral of King Edward VII of Great Britain, his unsuccessful campaign for the presidency in 1912, and a visit to a Hopi Indian reservation. Also, the Roosevelt funeral procession in 1919 was filmed extensively.

urban panoramas and street scenes of turn-of-the-century America to glimpses of life in Japan, Jerusalem, Mexico, Africa, and Beirut. The films in the Paper Print Collection recorded the Alaska gold rush, the San Francisco earthquake and fire, the Galveston, Texas, flood, numerous parades and processions, the beaches and amusement parks where Americans enjoyed newfound leisure time, and the great world fairs and expositions of the period. Film cameramen shot scenes of numerous wars—the Spanish-American, Boer, and Russo-Japanese, as well as the Boxer Rebellion. Sports events—ranging from world champion boxing bouts, to the America's Cup Races, to cock fights and dog fights—survive in the Paper Print Collection, as do images of great sports figures such as Christy Mathewson and Jack Johnson.

Though William McKinley was the first president whose public activities were recorded on film, Theodore Roosevelt was the first president whose life was extensively preserved in motion pictures. The Library's Theodore Roosevelt Collection was assembled by the Roosevelt Memorial Association, an organization chartered by an act of Congress on May 31, 1920. This collection was transferred to the Library of Congress in 1962. By the time of his death in 1919, Roosevelt's activities had been extensively documented through news films going

OPPOSITE. The Spanish-American War of 1898 was documented and celebrated in early films, such as those shown by traveling lecturer Lyman H. Howe. Lyman H. Howe poster, "Battle on Land." (*Motion Picture Posters Collection, Prints and Photographs Division*)

Such was the appetite of the public for actualities documenting public figures and events, that creative re-creations were sometimes passed off as the real thing. Recordings of Pres. William McKinley's last public address—delivered on September 5, 1901, at the Pan-American Exposition in Buffalo the day before he was shot by anarchist Leon Czolgosz—were marketed as "President McKinley's Last Speech." Early recordings aficionado Jim Walsh discovered that the brother of variety artist Len Spencer, Harry, actually made the recordings. A Columbia official later explained, "While we didn't say that the record was by McKinley, we were perfectly willing for the public to think it was, if that would increase sales." The MBRS Paper Print Collection includes a short actuality silent film of the real speech.

The A. F. R. Lawrence Collection, the 1974 gift of a CBS Records executive, contains many early historic speeches and radio broadcasts that document America in the early decades of the century. Included in the collection are recordings made by political figures from 1918 to 1920 in the *Nation's Forum* series, an effort to raise money for World War I and later to inform Americans of the issues of the 1920 presidential campaign. This series includes Franklin D. Roosevelt's earliest recording, a disc entitled "Americanism," recorded when he was the 1920 Democratic vice-presidential candidate. Users of the World Wide Web can listen to the Roosevelt recording and other *Nation's Forum* speeches at the Library's American Memory web site.

A particular strength of MBRS's collections is opera recordings. Through gift collections from such donors as John Secrist, Joseph B. Strohl, and Karl Bambach the Library holds nearly complete runs of discs by such greats as Enrico Caruso, John McCormack, and Rosa Ponselle. The Caruso "picture disc" was issued by Victor twelve years after his death, in 1933. A McCormack record was issued in 1932 to raise funds for a proposed cathedral in Liverpool.

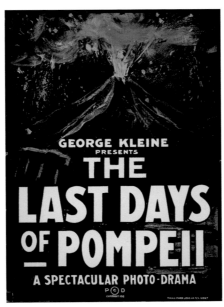

back to 1897, when, as Assistant Secretary of the Navy, he appeared in a brief film leaving the White House.

Although the Library acquired its first sound recording in 1906 (a cylinder recorded two years earlier by Prof. E. W. Scripture of Harvard University of Kaiser Wilhelm II reading a speech), it did not actively collect recordings until 1925, when the Victor Talking Machine Company began to donate selected recordings on an annual basis. Most of the Victor gifts were from their select "Red Seal" series. The Red Seal connoted talent of artistic distinction and marked a change in recorded talent from the earlier period of variety stars and military bands. Since 1903, Victor had recorded the great stars of opera, such as Ada Crossley, Antonio Scotti, Nellie Melba, and Geraldine Farrar. Victor's coup had come when it signed the new Metropolitan Opera tenor Enrico Caruso to an exclusive contract. From 1904 until 1920, as acoustical technology improved significantly, Caruso recorded exclusively for Victor. By the time of his death in 1921, Caruso had earned over two million dollars from recordings. Caruso's rise to international acclaim by a mass public can only be attributable to his Victor recording career; similarly, the rapid growth of the recording industry during this period was due in large part to the existence of such nascent superstars as Caruso. Beginning in the 1910s, the film industry also began to organize the production companies around stars the public flocked to see.

The most famous film star of the period was Mary Pickford—"America's Sweetheart"—who gave the Library its first major gift of motion pictures

During the formative years of the the studio system, a select group of women carved a niche for themselves as producers and directors, positions that would, for the most part, be off-limits to members of their sex throughout most of the sound era. Lois Weber (left), one of the most socially conscious filmmakers of her time, confers with renowned Russian ballerina Anna Pavlova (seated), on the set of the costume drama, *The Dumb Girl of Portici* (Universal Film Manufacturing Company, 1916). Weber's husband and codirector, Phillips Smalley, looks on at right.

Shirley Mason in *The Apple Tree Girl* (Thomas A. Edison, Inc., 1917; distributed by K-E-S-E Service). In addition to importing spectacular historical features, Kleine also distributed domestic products, including this "woman's picture," in which an ambitious orphan resolves to remake herself before going off in search of fame and fortune. (*George Kleine Collection, Moving Image Section*)

MACK SENNETT COMEDIES

The slapstick Mack Sennett studios spawned many of the great physical comedians of the silent era, including Charlie Chaplin, Buster Keaton, Fatty Arbuckle, and Mabel Normand. In this publicity still, cross-eyed favorite Ben Turpin cavorts with a bevy of Sennett bathing beauties.

following its decision in 1945 to create a motion picture repository. At one time, she vowed to destroy the early films in which she appeared. "So many of them were ridiculous, you know," she told a reporter in 1964. "I was afraid of becoming a laughingstock." Fortunately for future generations, her friend and fellow actress Lillian Gish convinced her that "they would be studied and appreciated in time."

The Pickford Collection contains approximately a hundred titles from the years when she made one-reelers with the Biograph Company from 1909 to 1912, to her later feature films, which display a range of acting styles and subtlety of performance rarely encountered in early films. Forty-nine of the fifty Biograph films, nearly all of which were acquired as original negatives, were directed by D. W. Griffith. Pickford gave the Library $10,000 for preservation efforts in 1956 and bequeathed in her will $500,000 to fund over a ten-year period the operations of a film theater housed in the Library. The Mary Pickford Theater, located in the Library's James Madison Building, was dedicated on May 10, 1983. Pickford, whose films will now live on for future generations to enjoy, expressed her appreciation of the Library's preservation efforts when she said, "Without you, many of my films would have turned to dust."

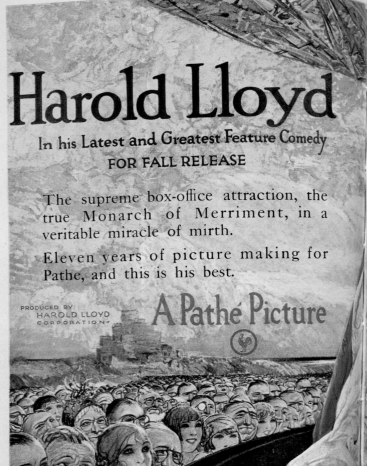

Harold Lloyd

In his Latest and Greatest Feature Comedy
FOR FALL RELEASE

The supreme box-office attraction, the true Monarch of Merriment, in a veritable miracle of mirth.

Eleven years of picture making for Pathe, and this is his best.

PRODUCED BY
HAROLD LLOYD
CORPORATION

A Pathé Picture

MICHELSON

Long films lasting over an hour, based on classical works, were being produced in Italy during the silent film era. A few American distributors took a gamble in acquiring some of these films and exhibiting them in legitimate houses. At the same time, in the trade press an attempt was made to distinguish these new features as works of high art for the "classes," as opposed to entertainment for the "masses." Progressive interests promoted features as tools for uplifting the masses, as they condemned the genres of crime, immorality, roughhouse comedy, and cowboys common to the single-reel film. Some stage stars saw the feature film as an opportunity to document their acting art for posterity.

In 1947, the Library of Congress purchased the motion picture-related holdings of the estate of George Kleine, the largest importer of foreign features and of shorter films in the United States and Canada until the beginning of World War I. "George Kleine in the old days was to the motion picture industry what John D. Rockefeller is to Standard Oil," wrote movie columnist Louella Parsons in 1923. Kleine began his career assisting in his father's optical store in Chicago. By 1908, advertisements from the Kleine Optical Company stated, "We control for America the entire output of films made by the most celebrated European factories." In 1913, Kleine imported from Italy *Quo Vadis?*, a two-and-a-quarter-hour spectacle of classical Rome. Booked by Cohan and Harris, a theatrical company, the film outdid legitimate theater in box office receipts in New York, Brooklyn, Chicago, Philadelphia, and Boston. With the success of *Quo Vadis?*, Kleine commissioned the Italian productions of *Othello* and *The Last Days of Pompeii*.

While the recording industry had fully matured by the 1920s—recording and marketing opera arias, symphonic music, ethnic music, jazz, and dance music—it suffered its first major setback in sales when radio began to be established as a rival home entertainment. Although early radio broadcasts include a 1910 performance by Caruso, sports events, election returns, weather reports, recorded music, and live dance bands, radio use was largely limited to professional and military use, and was enjoyed as a hobby by mostly youthful tinkerers during the twenty years after Marconi's 1901 trans-Atlantic transmission. In 1916, Marconi telegrapher David Sarnoff was not taken seriously when he set forth "a plan of development which would make radio a 'household utility' in the same sense as the piano or phonograph." In 1922, the truth of Sarnoff's prediction began to be felt—over five hundred new stations began broadcasting that year. By 1926, when the National Broadcasting Corporation formed the first national network with Sarnoff as head, 24 percent of American homes had a radio. By 1931, the figure had risen to 55 percent.

OPPOSITE. The shorts of slapstick pioneer filmmaker Hal Roach provided an arena of comic experimentation for such developing talents as Laurel and Hardy, Will Rogers, Harold Lloyd, and Charley Chase. The Roach stock company included such favorites as Snub Pollard, ZaSu Pitts, Bebe Daniels, Jean Harlow, Fay Wray, and Paulette Goddard. Soon-to-be directing giants George Stevens and Leo McCarey spent their journeyman years with Roach crafting skills in film comedy and storytelling that would serve them well throughout their long careers. Harold Lloyd, one of silent film's true kings of comedy, is pictured here in a 1925 trade paper advertisement.

Electrification of Sound

AUDIOVISUAL COLLECTIONS
BETWEEN THE WARS

OPPOSITE. Technical progress and the competitive nature of the industry have fostered a variety of audiovisual formats. One hundred years ago cylinders vied against discs for popularity; fifty years ago the public was asked to choose between 45rpm and 33rpm discs; only recently, the Betamax video tape format lost out to VHS. The Library's collections include unique materials in all of these formats, the losers in the format wars as well as the survivors. Since most of these formats were created for consumer use, long-term stability was not considered an important factor by their manufacturers, which has created special challenges for archives.

THE TECHNOLOGY developed during World War I that allowed radio to become a major medium of mass communication also brought profound changes to both the recording and film industries in the 1920s. The introduction of carbon microphones and amplifiers expanded the frequency range that could be reproduced on record. The equipment that Western Electric developed for radio broadcasting would, by the end of the decade, be used to create "talking pictures," an innovation that marked not only the end of the art of silent film, but also the birth of a new era in which sounds and pictures were merged to bring a greater sense of realism to film's documentation of the world and to form creative works that constituted a new art of the screen.

The era inaugurated by the electrification of sound recording and transmission began as America was passing through what F. Scott Fitzgerald called the "Jazz Age." Films, radio, and recordings were as integral a part of this period as literature. During the Great Depression that followed, these media continued to serve the mass audience in ways as diverse as those exemplified by Franklin Roosevelt's "Fireside chats" over the radio and the stunning Astaire-Rogers dance musicals of the 1930s. It was also during this period that the Library began systematically to amass the audiovisual materials of what has become the largest such collection in the world.

David Sarnoff's conception of wiring a group of stations to support national advertising and nationally directed, high-budget programming resulted in the birth of the National Broadcast Corporation (NBC) on November 15, 1926. Owned by the Radio Corporation of America, a company formed to pool the radio patents of Marconi, General Electric, Westinghouse, AT&T, and United Fruit, NBC's original two dozen or so stations grew to hundreds as the Red Network, and was joined in 1927 by a second, coast-to-coast web of stations called the Blue Network. (The U.S. Department of Justice would later force NBC to relinquish the Blue Network. It was sold in 1943 and became the American Broadcasting Company.)

The Library's NBC Collection comprises the most comprehensive publicly available broadcasting archive in the United States. The collection began in 1978 with the gift of 150,000 sixteen-inch lacquer-coated transcription discs—over a hundred thousand radio programs and television soundtracks dating from 1935 to 1971. The audio recordings were later supplemented by 18,000 kinescope reels of NBC television broadcasts. Papers and manuscripts donated include NBC's original set of "program analysis files," which describe almost every NBC radio program produced in New York City. The NBC master files at the Library include nearly fifteen hundred corporate files that outline the history of the network, supplying

significant documentation on over seventy years of commercial broadcasting in America. The files provide insight into the history of NBC's corporate policies, its technical achievements, and its World War II contributions. Tens of thousands of radio and television scripts are included in the master book component of the NBC Collection. While recordings of broadcasts from the early era of radio history are extremely rare, these textual resources of the NBC Collection contain an abundance of information about the period.

Audio and video highlights of the NBC Collection at the Library include kinescopes of NBC's unprecedented television opera productions, a complete record of the NBC Symphony (November 13, 1937–April 4, 1954), hundreds of *Huntley-Brinkley Reports*, and thousands of morale-boosting World War II–era radio broadcasts. Through the abundant documentation in the NBC Collection, we can recreate the sound of radio from seventy years ago, study the birth of television, and understand the development of commercial broadcasting and its oldest broadcasting network.

While the early history of recordings is documented thoroughly in the Library due to generous donors and tenacious collecting, most broadcasting from radio until the mid-1930s cannot be heard today for the simple reason that little was recorded. Live broadcasting that has survived from the 1920s was recorded for the most part on noisy aluminum discs. In the mid 1930s, quieter lacquer-coated discs were introduced, and although network policy during this period prohibited the use of recorded programs, transcription recordings of broadcasts began to be produced. The radio networks transcribed selected programs on a regular basis, and private transcription companies recorded radio shows for advertising clients and stars who appeared on the shows.

The Library started an Archive of Radio Recordings in fiscal year 1939. The Librarian's annual report indicated that, "As a result of an informal suggestion … the Columbia Broadcasting System has presented to the Library recordings of the most important musical performances broadcast by this network during the past year." The new archive obtained 468 transcription recordings, prepared by the Federal Music Project of the Works Progress Administration, which had been broadcast by non-network radio stations and many network radio programs from a commercial transcription service. During World War II, radio programs were dutifully transcribed by the Library, but systematic recording efforts ended at the war's conclusion.

The archive was revived in 1956 when General Foods, Incorporated donated 250 magnetic tapes of 21 programs and 130 scripts representing a broad spectrum

Early original audio recordings of radio are scare. However, the NBC Collection at the Library provides numerous means to study the content of early network broadcasting. NBC radio created daily compilations of its scripts, advertisements, and music licensing log sheets into clip-bound master books. The master books were microfilmed by NBC in the 1960s and the originals were destroyed. Shown here are one of the few existing original master books, dated November 15, 1936 (NBC's tenth anniversary), and the film representing the year 1936.

of programs they sponsored in the 1930s and 1940s, including *The Jack Benny Program*, *The Thin Man*, *Young Dr. Malone*, *Duffy's Tavern*, and *The Aldrich Family*, the first of many situation comedy series to focus on teenagers within the family circle. In succeeding years, the Library has acquired through donation and purchase a diverse collection of radio programs from these formative years.

It was during this period in radio that many of the types of programs emerged that today constitute much of television programming. The Library's collection includes variety shows hosted by celebrities and performers such as Al Jolson and Rudy Vallee; quiz shows, such as the popular *Information Please*; crime melodramas, like *The Shadow* and *Gang Busters*; dance music from the once-popular but now nearly forgotten Jack Arthur and his hotel orchestra; educational shows, such as *American School of the Air* and Walter Damrosch's *Music Appreciation Hour*; and the ever-present soap opera, which some historians suggest provided diversely situated American housewives with a mythic world of shared experience.

The Library's collection holds numerous selections from the great comedy shows of the era, such as *The Fred Allen Program*, *Burns & Allen*, and *Amos 'n' Andy*—for the last show, in addition to recorded broadcasts, the Library owns a complete script collection that resides in the Manuscript Division. The longest-running panel debate program, *The University of Chicago Round Table*, is well-represented in the Library. The Mary Margaret McBride Collection features over eleven

**MAJOR BOWES'
AMATEUR HOUR**

(Please print plainly in ink)

APPOINTMENT:
Theatre – 10/26
3 P.M.

FORM E 12M 8-39

POSSIBILITY FOR:
10/76/39

Name _Sills_ _Beverly_
　　　Last Name　　　First Name
New York Address _580 Empire Blvd Bklyn_
New York Telephone _SLb-8487_
　　　　　　　　Residence
Home Address _580 Empire Blvd Bklyn, N.Y._
　　　　　　City　　　　　State
Street Address _____
　　　　　　　　Home Telephone Number
How long do you intend to remain in New York? _____

Type of Entertainment: _I'm 10 years old. I'm studying singing_
Give facts of your vocations, Past and Present _with Miss Estelle Liebling_
and all Details of Interest: _I have 22 arias on my repertoire_
I have done 2 pictures with
Educational Films and have
appeared at many entertainments
Professional and Amateur.

List all Previous Radio
Appearances if any: _W.O.R. & W.M.C.A._

FOR AUDITION DEPARTMENT USE ONLY
(DO NOT FILL IN)

M. R. _A--1_　　D. R. _____
Date: OCT 25 1939　Auditioned by: _Shelby (Reed)_
Selection: _"Caro nome"_
Alternate: _____

The application from Beverly Sills to sing on Major Bowes's *Original Amateur Hour,* dated 1939, when she was ten. Sills is seen here in costume for Johann Strauss's *Die Fledermaus* for her farewell performance in 1980 in the New York City Opera production "A Lincoln Center Special: Beverly! Her Farewell Performance," broadcast on PBS. (*Photo by Richard Corkery, Biographical File, Prints and Photographs Division*)

hundred hours of McBride's weekday talk shows, a pioneering mixture of interviews, advice, and product plugging that attracted an average of six million listeners daily. Her guests from the worlds of politics, science, and the arts—including Jimmy Durante, Gertrude Lawrence, Edward Steichen, Eleanor Roosevelt, Ralph Ellison, and Gen. Omar Bradley—often opened up to her empathic and intelligent questioning and felt comfortable enough to speak about emotional and difficult subjects.

Over the years, the Library has acquired a number of special radio collections of importance from the "Golden Age." Jessica Dragonette, one of radio's most popular singing stars, presented to the Library over four hundred recordings of her radio shows on both the *Cities Service Concerts* and the *Palmolive Beauty Box Theatre,* in which she performed songs from operettas and musicals. Lewis Graham, producer of Major Bowes's *Original Amateur Hour,* one of radio's most popular shows, donated 2,200 discs of recordings from shows broadcast from its inception in 1935 to 1945. A number of the programs showcase the early talent of performers who later became prominent, such as Frank Sinatra, Beverly Sills, and, possibly, Maria Callas (her appearance under a pseudonym has not been authenticated.)

Also in the Library's collection are an abundant selection of CBS's *Columbia Workshop*, which presented original and sometimes experimental dramatic works, such as former Librarian of Congress Archibald MacLeish's 1937 radio play *The Fall of the City*, which featured a young Orson Welles in an eerie depiction of the fascist assault on a lethargic population. Many of the *Workshop* broadcasts were written and directed by Norman Corwin, one of the first masters of the medium. Orson Welles's acclaimed *Mercury Theatre of the Air* is represented by broadcasts such as *Dracula*, *Treasure Island*, *A Tale of Two Cities*, *Sherlock Holmes*, and, of course, the notorious 1938 presentation of H. G. Wells's *The War of the Worlds*, which panicked an incredulous public, who mistook the program's fictional on-the-spot reports of a Martian invasion of New Jersey for the real thing. The Library also has broadcasts of Welles's later *Campbell Playhouse* shows, including an October 1939 production starring Welles and Walter Huston of Booth Tarkington's novel, *The Magnificent Ambersons*. Three years later, Welles would make his film version of the novel and create one of the cinema's most treasured elegies to a bygone era.

The Library's collections additionally contain a wealth of 1920s and 1930s radio broadcasts of news coverage of important events, speeches—including presidential addresses to the nation—and discussions of issues. The Library's British Broadcasting Corporation Collection covers the "best of the BBC" broadcasts, preserved by the BBC on several thousand noncommercial, long-playing vinyl discs.

Finally, the Library's vast paper collections can help to fill in gaps in knowledge about radio from this era pertaining to broadcasts that were not recorded or have not survived. The rich CBS script collection in the Manuscript Division provides written texts for much of that network's output. The Library's runs of radio journals and trade papers can give researchers an understanding of this period from an industry insider's standpoint.

Although the recording industry adopted electrical apparatus to produce higher fidelity of sound recording than had been possible earlier with acoustical devices, sales of recordings plummeted as radio flourished in the 1920s. In the United States, $106 million were spent on recordings in 1921; by 1933, sales hit an industry low of $6 million. It was not until 1945 that record sales eclipsed the figures from the early 1920s. A number of record genres, though, grew strong during the twenties and thirties, even as sales declined for most of the others.

Record companies gave the term *race records* to discs they made for the

Seen here is conductor André Kostelanetz, who donated a substantial collection of recordings of his popular radio shows of the late 1930s and 1940s—The *Chesterfield Program, Tune-up Time*, and the *Coca-Cola Hour*. This collection includes unpublished off-the-air recordings featuring prominent soloists in unique performances, including violinists Mischa Elman, Yehudi Menuhin, and Nathan Milstein; pianists Oscar Levant and Alec Templeton; and vocalists Judy Garland, Grace Moore, Paul Robeson, and Lily Pons, who was also Kostelanetz's wife. (*André Kostelanetz Collection, Music Division*)

African-American market. The sale of race records was unaffected by the industry slowdown, but this seeming anomaly was actually a portent of a significant change in American culture that would eventually be felt throughout all audio-visual media. A preponderance of genteel "conservatory music," evidenced in the Library's collections of early acoustical records, gave way in the 1920s to jazz and other popular entertainment forms, as African-American culture began to spread through the North. The "race" market was discovered upon the 1921 release of Mamie Smith's "Crazy Blues," the first "vaudeville" blues recorded by an African American. It became an unexpected hit with both black and white buyers and led to the publication of tens of thousands of race records, which today are among the most sought after recordings by collectors and music lovers. In addition to female blues singers, race records contain jazz ensembles, gospel music and sermons, and rural blues, the last often recorded by record companies on field expeditions in the South. One 1927 Victor expedition to Bristol, Tennessee, resulted in the first recordings of the country legends Jimmie Rodgers and the Carter Family, among others. The next year Victor sent the Library a sample Rodgers disc, "Blue Yodel," with the explanation, "This record was released by us a month ago in the southern section of the country and met with instantaneous success. It has since proved to be one of our very best sellers. We thought you would be interested in hearing the type of music people are clamoring for today."

By mid-1938, the Library's audio holdings numbered only 4,156 records, most of which came from Victor. At this point, as part of a concerted effort to assemble a comprehensive collection of phonograph records, the Library induced the other major American record companies, notably Columbia and Decca, to donate their latest releases as gifts. In addition, the Library's Archive of American Folk-Song selected some three hundred race and hillbilly commercial records to add to their collections. The Library also began to collect records of national and folk music from other countries and recordings from a diverse number of ethnic groups within the United States.

The Depression brought about a drastic curtailment of race record sales, yet by the mid 1930s, a new form of big band jazz came on the scene that lent its name to the new era. As the Jazz Age died during the Depression, the Swing Era was born. Movies of the period had such titles as *Swing!*; *Swing High; Swing Low*; *Swing Your Lady*; *Swing It, Professor*; *Swing It, Sailor*; *Swing That Cheer*; and, of course, the Astaire-Rogers classic with its Gershwin score, *Swing Time*. The great swing bands of Benny Goodman, Glenn Miller, Tommy and Jimmy Dorsey, Fletcher Henderson, Harry James, and Teddy Wilson were just a few of the music makers

Before the beginning of widespread use of tape in the late 1940s, the 16-inch, lacquer-coated instantaneous disc was the standard format for recording radio broadcasts. Each disc side holds fifteen minutes of recording. At the Office of War Information radio studios in London during World War II, an archivist files away one of the many discs used in wartime broadcasting. The Library's collections include nearly three hundred thousand such discs. (*Office of War Information Collection, Prints and Photographs Division*)

combining African and European traditions to provide up-tempo rhythms and melodies to black and white dancers and listeners through radio, recordings, and films. The rise of the Swing Era was instrumental for the record industry's survival. With the end of Prohibition and the introduction of the jukebox in the newly opened taverns in the 1930s, the industry's comeback would be complete.

Outside of the commercial field, "unpublished" recordings were produced during this period for a variety of purposes. Folk music field recording expeditions sponsored by the Library of Congress have resulted in the documentation and preservation of an enormous corpus of indigenous music. The development of simplified on-the-spot, or instantaneous, recording techniques in the mid-1930s enabled the aural documentation of many aspects of American life. The Columbia University Brander Matthews Dramatic Museum Collection, a vast collection of speech recordings on discs from 1929 through 1936, includes many poets and writers reading from their own works and giving addresses, in addition to talks by political leaders, scientists, industrialists, and theatrical personalities. Some of the well-known personages represented in this collection include Presidents Hoover and Franklin D. Roosevelt, T. S. Eliot, Robert Frost, Jane Addams, Conrad Aiken,

OPPOSITE. From the turn of the century until after World War II, major record labels released recordings of ethnic music on 78rpm discs for sale to the new immigrant communities in the United States. By the early 1920s recordings for smaller labels, such as the Nofrio disc pictured, were appearing in greater numbers as well. Also pictured is a recording of popular Irish songs on the Columbia label, and the Mexican-American folk singer Lidya Mendoza's hit recording "Mal Hombre" for Bluebird.

An October 15, 1934, *Broadcasting* magazine advertisement for the Presto portable instantaneous disc recorder.

Heywood Broun, Amelia Earhart, Thomas Edison, Charles Evans Hughes, Aldous Huxley, Vachel Lindsay, Alfred E. Smith, Gertrude Stein, and Norman Thomas.

Instantaneous recording techniques enabled NBC to create its collection of radio broadcast transcriptions, now at the Library, and permitted smaller companies to contribute to radio broadcast content by creating programs locally and distributing them on mass-produced disc recordings. The C. P. MacGregor Company Collection of over six thousand recordings includes many transcription discs produced and distributed by the MacGregor Company in the 1930s and 1940s to radio stations. The discs feature such popular performers as the King Cole Trio, Stan Kenton and his Orchestra, Red Nichols and His Five Pennies, Jimmie Grier and His Orchestra, Peggy Lee, Anita Boyer, and Mel Tormé. The collection also contains 1,140 half-hour radio programs of the weekly dramatic series *Heartbreak Theatre*, sponsored by the Salvation Army and broadcast from 1956 to 1977.

As the recording industry increased the fidelity in recordings using electrical technology, and the radio became a fixture in homes across the nation, the movie industry embarked on serious experiments to combine sound with moving images. While sporadic attempts at producing sound films were made during the previous thirty years of film history, it was not until the mass American public became accustomed to high-fidelity aural entertainment in their homes that the necessary technological advances were achieved to accommodate in films the public's new taste for high quality recorded sound. In the 1920s, radio pioneer Lee De Forest, the inventor in 1906 of the audion tube, produced short sound films of vaudeville acts, operatic stars, and celebrities. These early experiments, many of which have been preserved in the MBRS collections, allow us today to experience the combined sounds and sights of popular entertainment as the era of vaudeville was drawing to a close. The De Forest films, donated by film and television producer Maurice Zouary, include acts of vaudeville headliners such as Eddie Cantor, Gallagher and Shean, Weber and Fields, Noble Sissle and Eubie Blake, Fanny Ward, DeWolf Hopper, and Sir Harry Lauder. The collection includes 1924 campaign speeches by candidates Calvin Coolidge, John W. Davis, and Robert M. LaFollette, and other public figures, including George Bernard Shaw and Charles Lindbergh.

Beginning in 1926, the Vitaphone Corporation, a Western Electric subsidiary, in collaboration with Warner Brothers, shot over eight hundred reels of film synchronized with sound recording discs of vaudeville performers, opera singers, and other popular acts of the time. The first public showing of the "Vitaphone" in New York on August 6, 1926, included the Overture from *Tannhäuser* performed by the New York Philharmonic Orchestra, concert violinist Mischa

Elman playing "Humoresque," Roy Smeck playing solo Hawaiian guitar and ukelele, and Metropolitan Opera tenor Giovanni Martinelli singing "Vesti la Giubba." The program "stirred a distinguished audience in Warners' Theatre to unusual enthusiasm," according to a *New York Times* reviewer, who predicted, "The future of this new contrivance is boundless." In 1927, when Al Jolson spoke lines of dialogue in the first feature with synchronized sound, *The Jazz Singer*, the country overwhelmingly approved, and the industry was transformed almost overnight. In the 1990s, the Library undertook to match Vitaphone discs to film in a project to restore these unique treasures.

As the film industry was completing its switch to sound in the late 1920s, the art of the silent film reached its peak with films like King Vidor's 1928 masterpiece *The Crowd*, which combined the best of silent film expressiveness with insights into group psychology and social relations rarely reached in any art form. Directors and cameramen had mastered silent film's expressive possibilities, writers had honed the creation of scene construction and composition of title card texts to a fine art, while actors had developed the knack of getting the most nuanced meanings out of gestures, glances, body movements, and facial expressions. The 1920s had seen epic productions like Douglas Fairbanks's *Robin Hood*, Cecil B. DeMille's *The Ten Commandments*, and James Cruze's *The Covered Wagon*; slapstick comedy in the work of Charles Chaplin, Buster Keaton, and Harold Lloyd; Jazz Age youth culture in the performances of Clara Bow and Louise Brooks and in films with such titles as *Our Dancing Daughters*, *The House of Youth*, *The Mad Whirl*, and

TOP LEFT. The 1923 De Forest Phonfilms "sound-on-film" production, featuring Noble Sissle and Eubie Blake in a recording of their vaudeville act, was created as an early experimental sound film four years before the exhibition of *The Jazz Singer*. *Sissle and Blake* has been released on video by the Library of Congress.

TOP RIGHT. This poster for a reissue of *The Jazz Singer* (1927) captures the historic moment in the film when Al Jolson sings Irving Berlin's "Blue Skies" to his adoring mother and ad-libs dialogue. With the addition of naturalistic sound to moving images, the "talkies" effectively challenged the ability of radio and recordings to present their public with musical and spoken-word performances. *(Warner Bros.)*

COMMENT ON THE PLAY

Audiovisual-related ephemera in the MBRS collections provide revealing glimpses into the popular culture of the past. This scrapbook from 1926 contains both a colorful cutout of screen idol Louise Brooks and an avid fan's comments concerning Brooks's latest film, *Love 'Em and Leave 'Em*.

The Perfect Flapper; sophisticated comedies of manners in the work of director Ernst Lubitsch; expressive visual dramas of Frank Borzage, F. W. Murnau, and Josef von Sternberg; ravishing romance melodramas with Rudolph Valentino and Greta Garbo; war dramas like King Vidor's *The Big Parade* and William Wellman's *Wings*; and an extreme naturalism in the decadently mannered films of Erich von Stroheim, such as *The Wedding March* and *Greed*.

The beginning years of sound film required a rebirth of camera and editing techniques, acting styles, and directing methods. Scores of stage directors, writers, and actors went West, along with journalists and tabloid writers who had an ear for slang and fast-paced dialogue. Sound film brought the movie musical to the forefront of 1930s entertainment, as the great popular composers and lyricists of Broadway—including Irving Berlin, George and Ira Gershwin, Jerome Kern, Oscar Hammerstein II, and Rodgers and Hart—directed their talents to the demands of the screen. Comedians of verbal wit, like the Marx Brothers, W. C. Fields, and Mae West, joined more traditionally visual masters like Laurel and Hardy in using dialogue in creatively humorous ways. The decade that began with gritty gangster dramas, like *Little Caesar* and *Scarface*, ended with extravaganzas like *The Wizard of Oz* and *Gone with the Wind*.

Although the Library did not acquire films during this period because of the dangers of storing nitrate films, it now holds extensive collections of films received directly from the major American studios covering the nitrate era. In general, the studio deposits consist of preprint material—original negatives; original soundtracks; and master positives, or fine grains, which, made from original negatives, are used to strike new prints. In many cases, the Library holds in its vaults the most original, pristine representations of studio films. The collections of Columbia, Disney, Paramount, RKO, Universal, and Warner Brothers films include over a thousand features and shorts produced for the most part between the late 1920s and early 1950s.

An important complement to the studio collections is a Library agreement with Turner Entertainment, which acquired the library of some thirty-three hundred films made by MGM, Warner Brothers, and RKO. By virtue of its arrangement with the Library, whenever a film in Turner's possession is colorized and submitted for copyright, the corporation sends a 35mm high-quality, black-and-white print of the original to the Library.

The Library not only has collected the studio releases, but over the years it has gathered a tremendous number of films made on the peripheries of the industry. The Library holds a number of important collections of footage from

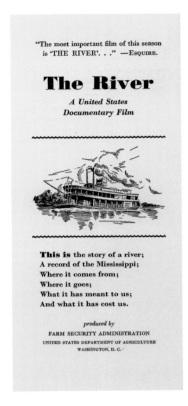

"The most important film of this season is 'THE RIVER'. . ." —ESQUIRE.

The River

*A United States
Documentary Film*

This is the story of a river;
A record of the Mississippi;
Where it comes from;
Where it goes;
What it has meant to us;
And what it has cost us.

produced by
FARM SECURITY ADMINISTRATION
UNITED STATES DEPARTMENT OF AGRICULTURE
WASHINGTON, D. C.

ethnographic and exploratory expeditions undertaken between the world wars, including those of Margaret Mead and Gregory Bateson to Bali and New Guinea; William O. Field to the Caucasus, Africa, and Moscow; Admiral Donald B. MacMillan to the Arctic regions of Greenland, Labrador, and the Hudson area; Osa and Martin Johnson to numerous regions around the world; Col. Herford Cowling to India, Southeast Asia, and Africa; and Julian Bryan to Russia. In 1996, the Library received material relating to the work of Pare Lorentz, the premier U.S. government filmmaker of the 1930s. Included in this collection are still photographs, scripts, publicity materials, and a print of *The River* that belonged to the editor of the film, Lloyd Nosler. Additional rare nonfiction films from this period in the Library's collections include footage taken by the American Relief Mission to Moscow during the famine of 1922 to 1924; *March of Time* newsfilms, beginning in 1932; films and raw footage from the radical Workers Film & Photo League; Burton Holmes films of the Chicago Century of Progress Exposition of 1933 to 1934; footage shot by the noted novelist, folklorist, and anthropologist Zora Neale Hurston; and the home movie collection of Jazz Age illustrator

The American documentary film movement gathered steam in the 1930s through films like *The City* (1939) (shown on the right), a collaboration of director-photographers Ralph Steiner and Willard Van Dyke, composer Aaron Copland, writer Lewis Mumford, and Pare Lorentz, who wrote the original outline. On the left is a publicity brochure from *The River.*

Ralph Barton, featuring personalities such as Sinclair Lewis, Anita Loos, Paul Robeson, Theodore Dreiser, and George Nathan.

During the period between the world wars, American racial and ethnic groups produced an array of films from within their own communities. The Library's collections are particularly strong in surviving African American films and in Yiddish films. Films such as Oscar Micheaux's *Within Our Gates* (1919), in part a response to the distorted portrayal of African Americans throughout mainstream films, present alternative visions of the black experience. The vibrant Yiddish cinema of the period, with films such as Maurice Schwartz's *Tevye*, a precursor to *Fiddler on the Roof*, brought much of the great Yiddish stage dramas to film, often with original casts.

The Library's largest collection of studio films, that of Columbia Pictures, comprises over four thousand features and shorts. Columbia, often characterized as one of the "Little Three" studios (along with United Artists and Universal) in contrast to the "Big Five" (MGM, Paramount, RKO, Twentieth Century–Fox, and Warner Brothers), is distinguished as the home of director Frank Capra for most of his career. The quintessential Capra hero—Gary Cooper in *Mr. Deeds*

In 1990, MBRS began a project to preserve and restore all of Frank Capra's films with funding provided by the David and Lucile Packard Foundation. The Library holds original negatives to seventeen of Capra's films, some of the most popular of which have suffered the worst deterioration. Only 60 percent of the original negative of *Mr. Smith Goes to Washington* (1939) survives. In this shot from the film's climactic scene set on the floor of the U.S. Senate, James Stewart nearly succumbs to the deviousness of demagogue politician Claude Rains. *(Copyright © 1939, renewed 1967 © Columbia Pictures, Inc. All Rights Reserved. Courtesy of Columbia Pictures)*

At last on the screen!

CABIN IN
THE SKY

What a Cast!

★ ETHEL WATERS
★ *Eddie* "ROCHESTER" *Anderson*
★ LENA HORNE
★ Louis Armstrong ★ Rex Ingram
★ Duke Ellington & His Orchestra
★ The Hall Johnson Choir

A
Metro-Goldwyn-Mayer
PICTURE

Goes to Town and *Meet John Doe*, and James Stewart in *Mr. Smith Goes to Washington*—plunges to the depths of disillusionment before taking action to combat the forces of big business and bureaucratic government that are at odds with traditional American communal ideals. Capra's patriotic vision would be particularly appropriate when he was chosen by Army Chief of Staff George C. Marshall following the American entry into World War II to head production on information films to provide some eight million new recruits with "answers as to *why* they are in uniform and *if* the answers they get are *worth* fighting and dying for," in the words of General Marshall. The resulting series of films, which came to be known as *Why We Fight*, remain persuasive exercises in political education.

In the days of legalized segregation, Hollywood produced a number of all-black-cast films. *Cabin in the Sky* (1943), featuring some of the great African-American entertainers of the period, was adapted from a Broadway show. The drawing in this lobby card is by Al Hirschfeld. (*Warner Bros.*)

37

"The Burden of This Education"

AUDIOVISUAL ACTIVISM
DURING WORLD WAR II

WHEN HE ASSUMED LEADERSHIP of the Library of Congress in 1939, Archibald MacLeish committed the institution to a national popular education policy. His goal was to combat the spread of fascism through widespread dissemination of materials demonstrating the appeal of a democratic way of life. Two enduring audiovisual legacies resulted from MacLeish's commitment to freedom: the establishment of the Library's Recording Laboratory, which enabled the Library to record and distribute the traditional oral heritage of America's diverse folk cultures, and the creation of a national "motion picture repository" that has become one of the great film archives in the world.

In a speech given in October 1939, entitled "Libraries and the Contemporary Crisis," MacLeish contended, "We will either educate the people of this Republic to know, and, therefore, to value and, therefore, to preserve their own democratic culture, or we will watch the people of this Republic trade their democratic culture for the nonculture, the obscurantism, the superstition, the brutality, the tyranny which is overrunning eastern and central and southern Europe." MacLeish argued that it was the job of American libraries to provide "the burden of this education." In this belief, he embarked on an activist course to take the lead in promoting popular education.

A week after this address, MacLeish applied to the Carnegie Corporation for funds so that the Library's collection of audio materials could be copied and circulated through libraries and broadcast over the radio. In April 1940, the Carnegie Corporation appropriated $41,520. The Recording Laboratory was established to record and copy for distribution music, stories, and other oral traditions of national and international folk culture. With soundproof studios, state-of-the-art phono-duplication facilities, a sound truck, and six portable recording machines, the Library's Recording Laboratory became the finest governmental recording facility in Washington. The Archive of Folk Song, which popular music columnist Robert Shelton, the rock critic, once deemed "The Fort Knox of the Folk Song," was established in 1928. The installation of the Recording Laboratory in 1940 enabled the Library to develop the collections further and share their wealth with the public.

In 1941, a grant from the Rockefeller Foundation supported the Library's production of a series of experimental popular educational radio programs, the Radio Research Project, using Recording Laboratory staff and facilities. Alan Lomax, from the Archive of Folk Song, oversaw one of the first instances of documentary radio in this project, as broadcasts were produced from such diverse sites as an "Okie" migrant camp in California, the Asheville Mountain Folk Festival,

OPPOSITE. Because of its outstanding facilities, the Library's Recording Laboratory often was utilized for sound-related war projects. Shown here in 1943 is a production team from the Office of Special Services, U.S. War Department. (*LC Archives, Series: Photographs, Illustrations, and Objects, Archive 2229, Manuscript Division*)

Robert Frost and Carl Sandburg are pictured here on May 2, 1950, in the Whittall Pavilion with Librarian of Congress L. Quincy Mumford. Clifton Fadiman wrote that the Library's collection "is probably the most systematic attempt yet made to capture in sound the visions of those who 200 years hence may be for our descendants what Milton, Keats, and Whitman are for us." (*Biographical File, Prints and Photographs Division*)

a TVA project in Georgia, and a traveling carnival. Resources in the Library's vast manuscript and local history collections were used in an early example of dramatized "people's history," a series conceived by Alexander Woollcott. Talent employed in the project included actors Walter Huston, Douglas Fairbanks, Jr., Raymond Massey, and Agnes Moorehead; writer Arthur Miller; and composer Earl Robinson. In the days following the attack on Pearl Harbor, the project recorded hours of interviews in ten locations across the nation to get the reactions of a varied group of Americans to their president's declaration of war.

Since 1941, the Library has produced recordings of poetry readings in the Recording Laboratory. The initial 1941–1942 poetry season included readings by Robert Frost, Carl Sandburg, Robertson Jeffers, and Stephen Vincent Benet.

From these and later recording sessions, the Library has issued spoken-word recordings of eminent poets and authors such as T. S. Eliot, Marianne Moore, W. H. Auden, Wallace Stevens, Gabriela Mistral, e. e. cummings, Robert Lowell, and H. L. Mencken.

During World War II, the Recording Laboratory cooperated with the U.S. Marine Corps to provide equipment, training, and consultation for the Marines to record material during battle for broadcasting. The unedited material from such battlegrounds as the Solomon Islands, Bougainville, and Saipan has become part of the Library's collection, as have hundreds of interviews with Marine Corps soldiers describing their combat experiences.

It was during World War II that the Library committed itself to establishing an archive of motion pictures. During the first half century of moviemaking, films deposited at the Library for copyright purposes had been examined summarily and quickly returned to their owners. Without facilities to store highly flammable nitrate film, the Library could not attempt to build a film archive. In a report to Congress in 1942, Librarian of Congress Archibald MacLeish lamented, "The national collection of motion pictures which should exist does not exist." To remedy this, on May 26 of that year a new policy was enacted whereby selected films submitted for copyright deposit would become part of the Library's permanent collection. With a grant from the Rockefeller Foundation, the Library, in collaboration with the Museum of Modern Art (MOMA), took the first steps that have led to the accumulation of one of the world's great film collections.

In his report to Congress, MacLeish clearly set out the principles that were to govern the acquisition of films for inclusion in the national collection. "It cannot be too emphatically stated," he wrote, "that the canons governing the Library's selection are in no sense based upon an attempt to secure the 'best' films released during the year." The underlying object, in the words of one of MOMA's staff, was to "serve the student of history rather than the student of the movie art," and thus to establish "a collection that will illuminate in retrospect the periods which have produced the films." At the end of this initial endeavor, acting Librarian of Congress, Luther H. Evans, announced on June 3, 1945, the creation of a "motion picture repository" at the Library, "to preserve those films which most faithfully record in one way or another the contemporary life and tastes and preferences of the American people."

In 1942, the American Federation of Musicians, under president James Caesar Petrillo, instituted a ban on union members making records until the union's demand for a royalty on all sound recordings sold was met. By mid-1943, with Decca Records leading the way, most record companies agreed to pay the musicians' union a small royalty. The two largest companies, Victor and Columbia, however, would hold out until late 1944. Jack Kapp, the founder of American Decca Records, collected cartoons related to the phonograph, which were donated to the Library after his death in 1949. This 1944 editorial cartoon is by Fred L. Packer. (*Courtesy of the* New York Daily News)

"Purchased at a Heavy Price"

OPPOSITE. An evaluation of the captured German material by the U.S. Army contains the following summary of its significance: "The value of the Nazi newsreel, perhaps the only reliable record of the Nazi times from the Nazi viewpoint, cannot be exaggerated. Study of the feature films will reveal the methods used to break down the resistance of the opposition, to glorify totalitarian morals and ethics, to prepare the population for antiracial legislation and the gas chamber, (and) to arouse the population to last ditch resistance … The documentary films supply the details of the methods used to put and to keep the people under control." (*Color press book from* Sieg im Westen (*Victory in the West, OKH, 1941), German Collection, Moving Image Section*)

THE LIBRARY BECAME A STOREHOUSE for captured World War II enemy audiovisual material when it began to accept custody of a substantial number of German, Italian, and Japanese motion pictures that had been confiscated. Following the attack on Pearl Harbor, the FBI seized property of enemy aliens from domestic film distributors. The U.S. Army later captured a large Third Reich collection in Bavaria. Transfers of motion pictures from other government agencies continued after the war. A 1946 report concerning the captured material stated, "No war has been so well documented as this one, and these film records will be of vital interest to historians who will want, later, to evaluate the forces of this important period of world history." It soberly noted, "The pictorial evidence accumulated during the war has been purchased at a heavy price in both money and lives."

The German Collection of captured films contains over twenty-eight million feet of film, including approximately a thousand silent and sound features produced between 1919 and 1945; over a thousand newsreels, including an extensive run of *Die Deutsche Wochenschau*, the Third Reich's weekly newsreel, dating from September 1939 to March 1945; and numerous educational, entertainment, documentary, and propaganda shorts. Nazi era films include Leni Riefenstahl's documentaries—*Triumph of the Will*, covering the Nuremberg Party Rally of 1934, and *Olympiad*, on the Berlin Olympics of 1936—*Jud Süss*, *Die Rothschilds*, and *Titanic*, a version that depicted a cowardly English crew and heroic German passengers in steerage. The collection also contains some of the masterpieces from the period of the Weimar Republic, including G. W. Pabst's version of the Bertholt Brecht–Kurt Weill musical *The Threepenny Opera*, Walter Ruttmann's *Berlin*, and Fritz Lang's films *Doktor Mabuse*, *M*, and *Die Nibelungen*.

The Italian Collection contains 40 features produced between 1934 and 1940; 275 Instituto Luce newsreels released between 1938 and 1943; and 100 Luce shorts issued from 1930 to 1943. The features have attracted the interest of scholars, as prints of these films have otherwise been difficult to locate. The collection includes numerous *telefoni bianchi* or "white telephone" movies, a genre prevalent in the fascist 1930s in which luxury, ease, and escapism predominate. The great tenor Beniamino Gigli stars in *Legittima Defesa*. Among the rarer items are some of the films that future neorealist directors, such as Roberto Rossellini, made at the end of the fascist period.

The Japanese Collection consists of 200 features and 700 educational, documentary, and propaganda shorts from the 1930s and the early 1940s, including newsreels *Asahi News* from 1935 to 1939, *Yomiuri News* from 1936 to 1940, and *Nippon News* from 1940 to 1945. The Japanese documentary material features full-length films of Japanese victories in Singapore, Malaysia, and the Philippines. Feature films within the Japanese Collection have gained the interest of many film scholars because they include early films of renowned directors, such as Akira Kurosawa's *Ichiban Utsukushiku* (The Shining Moment, 1944) and Yasujiro Ozu's only short, *Kagami Jishi*, which shows Kikugoro VI performing the famous Kabuki dance of the same name.

The Library returned the intellectual property rights of confiscated films in its possession to their countries of origin in 1963, in accordance with laws passed by Congress. In addition, the Library repatriated seized nitrate film after creating 16mm copies on safety stock.

Seized enemy sound recordings have also been preserved by the Library. Among the confiscated materials are propaganda speeches by Lord Haw-Haw and Axis Sally, which were broadcast from Germany during the war; a series of recordings concerning deliberations of the Armistice Commission as it settled fine points of the Franco-German armistice of 1940; speeches broadcast to Germany by the National Committee of Free Germany (Germans captured by the Russians), urging the Germans to overthrow Hitler; Goebbels's speech to the German people after the July 20, 1944, attempt on Hitler's life; and broadcasts by the Germans in North Africa to American soldiers, urging them not to fight for Roosevelt and the Jews.

Office of War Information Collection

THE OFFICE OF WAR INFORMATION (OWI) was the primary U.S. government agency sending propaganda abroad during World War II. Target audiences were Americans fighting overseas and all foreign countries involved in the conflict. A large part of this broadcasting collection is in foreign languages, including German, French, Italian, Japanese, Chinese, Tagalog, and Siamese. English-language material includes much American network radio broadcasting that is not known to have survived elsewhere.

In the early years, OWI manifested a liberal slant on American policy that often set it at odds with the State Department. This was evident when the Fascist Grand Council deposed Mussolini on July 25, 1943, and the King of Italy, Victor Emmanuel III, having regained power, made Marshal Pietro Badoglio prime minister. Outraged, OWI produced a broadcast declaring that the United States would never support "the moronic little King." The State Department, meanwhile, backed Badoglio hoping that his rule would help get Italy out of the war early. As a result of the broadcast, there was an uproar in Congress about who was in charge of foreign policy, and the editorial content of the OWI became more tightly controlled. A recording of the offending broadcast is in the OWI Collection.

The program *News from Home* consists of local news shows originally broadcast from stations across America and subsequently rebroadcast to troops overseas so that they could hear news from their communities. Broadcasts include a range of reports on such subjects as the effect of the black-out on a small town in New England, the U.S. Army takeover of a local prison in Columbus, and the enlistment of a whole baseball team in Rapid City. Highlights include Red Barber doing sports, the CBS Symphony conducted by Bernard Herrmann, William L. Shirer reporting news on CBS, shows for Russian Relief, an NAACP meeting from 1942, and live coverage from Algiers after the North African invasion.

OPPOSITE. The Library has a great number of transcriptions made by U.S. government agencies during World War II. Pictured here is a rehearsal from the Office of War Information's Office of Emergency Management-produced series *You Can't Do Business with Hitler*.

BELOW. During the war years, the Office of War Information film unit produced a motion picture on the Library of Congress. Pictured here is the Budapest String Quartet in the Coolidge Auditorium. The Recording Laboratory has recorded Music Division concerts for the permanent collections since 1940. The laboratory's work has contributed to broadcasts of the concerts for over fifty years.

The Invisible Highway Abroad

Lana Turner and Bob Hope respond to a fan's request to hear a steak sizzling on *Command Performance, U.S.A,* a popular Armed Forces Radio Service program based on soldiers' personal requests.

AT THE HEIGHT OF ITS OPERATIONS during World War II, the Armed Forces Radio Service (AFRS, later the Armed Forces Radio and Television Service, AFRTS) provided over fifty hours of programming a week to American troops, using both transcription discs and shortwave broadcasts of direct programming. Each month 83,000 discs were shipped from the United States to AFRS transmitters located throughout the world. In 1945, forty-three programs, comprising fourteen hours of material, were produced weekly for American forces. In addition, thirty-six hours a week of American commercial radio were distributed to overseas outlets. Supplementing land-based stations were hundreds of closed-circuit systems for use on ships and in hospitals. The mission was to educate, inform, and entertain. Today, AFRTS continues to operate under the programming philosophies conceived during World War II.

In July 1966, jazz critic Ralph J. Gleason wrote a syndicated column concerning rumors of a plan to destroy approximately fifty thousand AFRTS 16-inch radio transcription discs because of a shortage of space in storage facilities in Europe. Calling the discs "the greatest treasure trove of performances in history," Gleason noted that they included countless live performances of great jazz bands, including those of Count Basie, Woody Herman, Duke Ellington, and Fletcher Henderson; other gems, such as Nat "King" Cole broadcasts from a Hollywood nightclub featuring the West Coast debut of the Charlie Parker–Dizzy Gillespie group, with Milt Jackson; and twenty half-hour transcriptions of Billy Eckstine's big band from the late 1940s, which only produced a small number commercial discs.

After record collectors and other interested parties protested against the plan of destruction in letters to the U.S. Army, Congress, and other government officials, Gleason voiced an optimistic hope: "It might even be possible for a determined Congressman to arrange to have this material, by agreement with publishers and musicians, placed in some sort of a national archive." In response to this call, Sen. Robert F. Kennedy stepped in to facilitate the acquisition of these priceless recordings by the Library, which had been collecting selected AFRS records since November 1945. As a result of Senator Kennedy's efforts, the Library began to receive what was to become a flood of transcription recordings that were no longer needed for daily broadcasting at AFRTS stations around the world. Subsequently, the Library was placed on the mailing list to receive copies of all new transcription recordings as they were created and circulated. Today the Armed Forces Radio Collection constitutes the largest archive of American commercial radio broadcasts in MBRS. In addition to the intrinsic importance of music gathered here, the collection can be used to evaluate the functions of the service as a medium for promoting troop morale during wartime.

Postwar Boom

WHILE THE WORLD AT LARGE adjusted to the transformations of postwar life, the world of media underwent a series of technological revolutions that led to new modes of producing sounds and images, additional ways to entertain and inform its ever growing audiences, and novel forms for the creation of art works and cultural products. Postwar America witnessed the contemporaneous births of network television, the long-playing record, the "45," high fidelity and stereophonic sound, magnetic tape recording, Cinemascope, 3-D, Cinerama, and FM radio. New styles of jazz emerged, as did rhythm and blues, and rock and roll. Television brought an array of culture, now visual as well as aural, into private homes. To induce people to leave their TV sets and return to theaters, motion pictures expanded to protracted lengths, panoramic widths, and spectacular breadths, switched their norm from black-and-white to color, and offered franker treatments of sexual subjects than was allowable on the strictly family-oriented medium of television. A vibrant youth culture expressing values and lifestyles that challenged and worried older generations used the media as an integral force for self-identification. In turn, the young were exploited by the media to create new markets for their products.

Danny Kaye, one of the great funnymen of our time, with Pier Angeli in the 1958 film *Merry Andrew*. The Danny Kaye and Sylvia Fine Kaye Collection documents much of Kaye's television career and includes a large number of personal papers relating to the shows.

The Voice
of America

Many of the music recordings made by the Voice of America (VOA) that are now at the Library are unique recordings. In 1962, Leonard Bernstein and the New York Philharmonic performed Brahms's First Piano Concerto with Glenn Gould as the soloist. Gould's insistence on a very slow tempo led Maestro Bernstein to publicly disavow the interpretation before the live performance. A Library of Congress VOA tape was the source material for this 1998 first commercial release of the performance. *(Photo by Richard Avedon; Copyright © 1961 Richard Avedon. All Rights Reserved)*

AS POSTWAR INTERNATIONAL RELATIONS froze into the protracted, strained conflict that defined the age, media culture, especially radio, played an integral political role. Although the Voice of America (VOA) was born during World War II, it remained a forceful tool in the Cold War to promote American values and culture in communist-run countries. The VOA penetrated the Iron Curtain with radio waves daily, spreading news and views untainted by communist propaganda or censorship. In addition to information, the VOA broadcast musical programs to expose the vitality of American culture to parts of the world from which it was being excluded for ideological reasons. Musical performances by major figures in the jazz and classical worlds were recorded for VOA broadcasts. In the mid-1960s, the Library of Congress became a repository for these programs, many of which never had been broadcast in the United States.

The collection of over fifty thousand VOA recordings, dating from 1945 to the present, features U.S. symphony orchestras, such as the New York Philharmonic, the Philadelphia Orchestra, the Oklahoma Symphony Orchestra, and the Louisville Orchestra; recitals by virtuoso performers, such as Jascha Heifetz, James Melton, Ezio Pinza, and Maggie Teyte; performances from the Metropolitan Opera; and classical works by a broad range of U.S. composers, including Carlisle Floyd, George W. Chadwick, Paul Creston, Roy Harris, Walter Piston, William Grant Still, and Randall Thompson. Programs in the collection document such consequential cultural events as the Newport Folk Festival and the National Folk Festival. VOA recordings of the Newport Jazz Festival and the Monterey Jazz Festival significantly augment the Library's abundant collections of historic live jazz.

All That Jazz

JAZZ UNDERWENT CONSIDERABLE SHIFTS during the postwar period, its leaders giving birth to such diverse styles as bebop, "cool" jazz, and "free" jazz. The Library's rich collection charts this multifarious history through many of its nuanced developments. The collection of jazz recordings in the Library is one of the world's largest, most comprehensive, and most significant. Congress itself acknowledged the great value of this uniquely American art form when it passed a resolution in 1987 affirming that jazz "is hereby designated as a rare and valuable American treasure to which we should devote our attention, support, and resources to make certain it is preserved, understood, and promulgated." Congress recognized that jazz "is a unique force, bridging cultural differences in our diverse society," and noted that it has become "a true international language adopted by musicians around the world as a music best able to express contemporary realities from a personal perspective."

The Library's commitment to collecting and preserving jazz began long before this declaration of congressional appreciation. In 1938, Alan Lomax, director of the Library's Archive of American Folk Song, broke new ground in documentary recording by bringing New Orleans pianist, composer, and band-leader Ferdinand "Jelly Roll" Morton to the Library's Coolidge Auditorium for a series of interviews and musical performances, one of the first oral histories that was recorded phonographically. Lomax produced over seven hours of 78 rpm discs that captured the insights and artistry of a seminal creative force. Morton, a pioneer innovator who played ragtime in New Orleans when the century was new, made his first recordings in 1923. Through stories related in the Coolidge Auditorium that often incorporated piano playing, Morton returned to those early days in discussions of his life and the origins, styles, and theories of jazz.

In 1991, MBRS acquired two outstanding collections of jazz recordings that sweepingly document a period beginning before Morton's first recordings and

The Nesuhi Ertegun "Jelly Roll" Morton Collection includes all of Morton's commercial 78 rpm releases, in addition to test pressings, alternate takes, and radio programs that featured Morton. It was the gift of Time-Warner, Inc. and Ahmet Ertegun, cofounder of Atlantic Records, a pioneering label that specialized in jazz and rhythm and blues. The 1993 gift of Morton's recordings was made in honor of Ertegun's brother Nesuhi, a key producer instrumental in the revival of traditional jazz in the 1950s and an avid enthusiast for the music of Morton.

Jazz and blues 78 rpm discs issued in the 1920s.

Among the Duke Ellington unpublished recordings included in the Valburn-Ellington Collection are several radio broadcasts made by Ellington from the Hurricane Club in New York City. Gordon Parks documented Ellington's stint at the nightclub for the Office of War Information. This photograph is one of seventy-four taken by Parks. (*FSA/OWI Collection, Prints and Photographs Division*)

continuing through the early years of the postwar era: The Robert Altshuler Collection and the Valburn-Ellington Collection. The Altshuler Collection of 250,000 78rpm records spans the years 1917 to approximately 1950 and is a primary source for inquiry into musical influences. The 78rpm format common to this era required musicians to render a complete emotional and aesthetic musical statement within a three- to four-minute time frame. The time constraint posed a challenge for artists to convey the vitality of original, improvised performances in a compressed format. The rich legacy preserved in the Altshuler Collection exhibits striking evidence of the creative responses jazz artists devised within the disciplined confines of the recording studio. A variety of jazz styles evolved as 78s became the medium of musical exchange not only for afficionados, but for jazz artists themselves, as they studied and emulated the great sounds and compositional ideas they heard on the phonograph and radio.

The Valburn-Ellington Collection, acquired by the Library from jazz connoisseur Jerry Valburn, includes approximately three thousand 78rpm discs, five thousand LPs, and three thousand unpublished, open-reel tapes of Edward Kennedy "Duke" Ellington. Every known commercially released 78rpm recording made by Duke Ellington is represented here in its original format, with one exception—a shellac Blu-Disc present in facsimile. The collection includes unpublished recordings created by record producer and sound engineer Jerry Valburn. Holdings

The MBRS Division's Motion Picture Conservation Center recently made a new archival print of the award-winning 1944 short *Jammim' the Blues*, directed by *Life Magazine* photographer Gjon Mili, which features Lester Young, Illinois Jacquet, Sweets Edison, and Jo Jones. *(Warner Bros.)*

begin with Ellington's first recording, "It's Gonna Be a Cold, Cold Winter," made in late 1924, and conclude with a 16mm color film of the composer's funeral in 1974. A short 1937 newsreel feature entitled *Record-Making with Duke Ellington* traces the process of manufacturing a record using the Duke Ellington Orchestra as its example. Another short, *Symphony in Black*, examines Ellington's musical themes and presents a then little-known singer named Billie Holiday.

Jazz recordings have come to MBRS from many diverse sources. The NBC Radio Collection includes unpublished broadcasts by Count Basie, Ella Fitzgerald, Benny Goodman, and Charlie Parker. One collection, that from Wally Heider, focuses on swing and West Coast jazz performances, highlighted by those captured on tape by recording engineer Heider in the 1950s and 1960s. The Wally Heider Collection also includes several thousand performances on "electrical transcription," or ETs, the broadcasting industry term for recordings created to be played on the radio. The Frederic Klinger Collection includes over forty thousand jazz long-playing discs, nearly every jazz recording issued in this format.

MBRS jazz holdings do not end with recordings. Performances of renowned artists such as Louis Armstrong, Duke Ellington, Thelonious Monk, and Miles Davis can be seen in over six hundred feature films, documentaries, and kinescopes of old television broadcasts that reside in the division's collections. Jazz-related moving images range from the 1923 sound film of Noble Sissle and Eubie Blake to rare Japanese laser discs of Sonny Rollins and Dizzy Gillespie.

LPs, 45s, and Magnetic Tape

Ａ́ltHOUGH JAZZ ARTISTS creatively adjusted to recording on 78 rpm discs, the time limitations of the format for classical works had long been felt to be constraining. Multiple-disc albums required listeners to interrupt classical pieces three to five times in order to change records. Although experimentation with "Long Playing" discs took place as early as 1926, the Depression and war that followed held up the research necessary to perfect a new process.

In 1949, consumers had a choice of three record formats: 78 rpm (upper left), 45 rpm (lower left); and 33⅓ rpm long-playing records. (Science Illustrated *photo by Dick Wolters, Specific Subject File, Prints and Photographs Division*)

RUSSELL

WOOLLEN

TRIPTYCH

QUARTET FOR FLUTE & STRINGS

WILSON

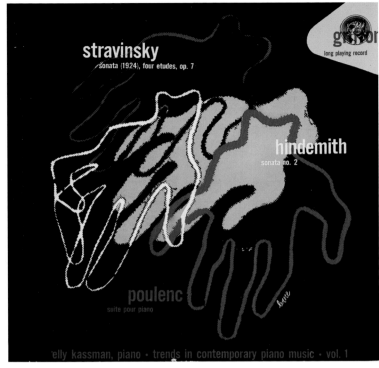

stravinsky
sonata (1924), four etudes, op. 7

hindemith
sonata no. 2

poulenc
suite pour piano

elly kassman, piano · trends in contemporary piano music · vol. 1

long playing record

stockhausen
aus den sieben tagen · from the seven days · venu des sept jours

Deutsche Grammophon

ANTHOLOGIE DE MUSIQUE RITUELLE
MAÇONNIQUE CONTEMPORAINE

Pierre Max
DUBOIS

orchestre
sous
la direction
de l'auteur

Fred ZELLER

RCA VICTOR

STEREO 540.059 M

In June 1948, Columbia publicly demonstrated a 12-inch microgroove disc that played for up to twenty-four minutes per side at 33⅓ rpm, a speed first used in the 1920s for the production of Vitaphone motion picture sound discs. The new disc, or "LP," was made of unbreakable vinyl, a polyester plastic developed during the war as an alternative to shellac, the 78 rpm base. Supplies of shellac had dried up during a Japanese blockade of Malaysia. Vinyl pressings produced much less surface noise than shellac discs; the new format provided a broad frequency range for high fidelity sound quality. Shortly after 1948, RCA Victor introduced the 7-inch 45 rpm microgroove disc that played for about the same amount of time as a 78, but was less expensive and also quieter.

The new formats led to another "format war," similar to that between cylinders and discs at the beginning of the century. The brief "War of the Speeds" ensued between corporate interests vested in the competing products. The conflict ended when the two new formats began to be delegated to different types of music. LPs were used primarily for classical works and albums of popular songs. Forty-fives, as the format of choice for the releasing of individual songs, soon found its niche with the growing youth culture of the 1950s. At first 78s were relegated to the children's market; by the end of the fifties, they had virtually disappeared.

As these new record formats were developing, experimentation was proceeding with magnetic tape recording technology, the results of which would alter production methods of not just the recording industry, but radio, television, and eventually, motion pictures. Audio tape recorders had been developed in Germany during World War II. In 1947, Bing Crosby popularized the use of tape when he began to record his radio shows for network broadcast so that he could edit the shows for quality control. Audio tape soon replaced the disc in recording studios and also began to be used extensively in noncommercial settings due to its relatively easy operating procedures and superior sound quality.

Tape recorders could be of great aid to composers and influenced the manner in which some musicians created. They were crucial to the work of electronic music composers, such as Vladimir Ussachevsky, who composed new works with tape recorders as the performing medium. Jazz musicians, such as Gerry Mulligan and Milt Hinton, harnessed the convenience of tape recorders to record rehearsal and recording sessions for personal evaluation at a later time. The tape collections of both of these music pioneers are now in the care of MBRS. Tape also simplified and encouraged aural documentation. In 1952, the National Press Club initiated a taping program of addresses and question-and-answer sessions of its distinguished luncheon and evening guests. The Library's collection of nearly two

Newer magnetic media, such as audio and video tape, pose great challenges to archives. Heat and humidity are the chief enemies of tape. The chemical composition of some types of magnetic tapes causes them to absorb moisture, thereby rendering them unplayable after time. Eventually, all tapes suffering from "sticky-tape syndrome," as the condition is termed, must be dried out and recopied. Here tapes are being baked at a low temperature in preparation for preservation duplication.

OPPOSITE. The Library has received its collection of twentieth-century classical music albums from diverse sources, including copyright deposit and private collectors. Pictured here are Russell Woollen's "Quartet for Flute and Strings" on the cutting edge Transition label (circa 1955); pianist Elly Kassman performing Stravinsky, Hindemith, and Poulenc on the rare Griffon label (1950); the very rare Karlheinz Stockhausen "Aus den Sieben Tagen" on Deutsche Grammophon (1973); and Pierre Max Dubois's "Anthologie de Musique Rituelle Maçonnique Contemporaine," made in France by RCA (1966).

thousand National Press Club recordings includes speeches and discussions by presidents, foreign leaders, congressmen, cabinet members, and cultural figures. Other significant tape collections in MBRS include the J. Robert Oppenheimer Collection composed of over seventy recordings of Dr. Oppenheimer's lectures and interviews from the 1950s and 1960s, some of which were recorded on tape; musical performances recorded at the White House; a 1968 gift from the American International Music Fund of tape recordings of new works by known and yet-to-be-discovered composers; interviews with composers, such as Aaron Copland and Alberto Ginastera, about the creation of individual works; and a series of lectures by eminent psychiatrists.

The introduction into the industry of magnetic tape recording technology allowed a multitude of small companies to produce good quality LPs and 45s inexpensively and compete successfully against the established giants by concentrating on niche markets like country music or rhythm and blues. The quantities of product released by these new companies created acquisition challenges for the Library. Established agreements had been set up with the major corporations whereby new releases would be sent to the Library, but channels had not been set up to keep up with the new releases coming from the influx of independent companies. However, in the 1950s the Library began to catalog sound recordings, and smaller companies sent new releases to the Library for cataloging. In addition, the Library has acquired a number of significant special collections in the new formats. The Stephen Sondheim, William J. Doran, J. Thomas and Laurence Rimer, and Keith Fleming LP collections of classical music fill in crucial gaps in LC's holdings of discs released before the 1972 copyright deposit regulations and of important foreign issues.

In addition to affecting the type of records produced in the studio, the introduction of magnetic tape enhanced the roles of the record artist, producer, and studio engineer. In the 1950s, Frank Sinatra, working with arranger Nelson Riddle, used the LP format to create ambitious "concept" albums in which the tones and shadings of individual songs combined to create moods that moved throughout the albums. Innovative use of the LP in popular music would reach new heights in the 1960s when artists such as Bob Dylan, the Beatles, the Beach Boys, and Jimi Hendrix experimented with complex, unified, aural experiences. The vast influence of magnetic tape was by no means limited to audio. In the 1950s, tape recorders were created to record and play back images as well as sounds, leading to videotape usage in television production and later the birth of the video cassette recorder (VCR) and the introduction into the home of tape recording and viewing.

ABOVE AND OPPOSITE. Concept albums in MBRS include Frank Sinatra's *In the Wee Small Hours* (1955); Les Baxter's *Space Escapade* (1958), in which all the selections have space themes; The Mothers of Invention's *Absolutely Free* (1967), in which each side has a separate title and theme; Genesis's *The Lamb Lies Down on Broadway* (1974), one of the last of the first wave of rock concept albums, and one of the best; and Parliament's *Funkentelechy vs. The Placebo Syndrome* (1977), produced and conceived by George Clinton. (Absolutely Free, *Verve Records.* The Lamb Lies Down on Broadway, *Atlantic Recording Company.* Funkentelechy vs. The Placebo Syndrome, *Casablanca Record and Film Works, Inc.*)

SPACE ESCAPADE
LES BAXTER

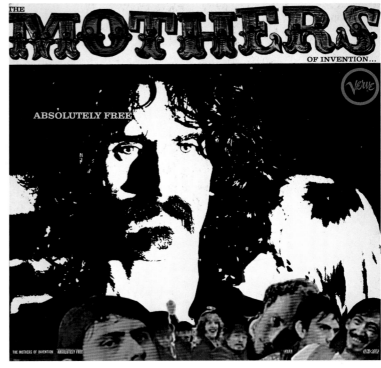

THE MOTHERS
OF INVENTION...

ABSOLUTELY FREE

GENESIS
THE LAMB LIES DOWN ON BROADWAY

N 19639 1974

PARLIAMENT
FUNKENTELECHY

SR 2-190

VS.
THE PLACEBO SYNDROME

TV

Although live television broadcasting was demonstrated in the 1920s, regular service did not begin in this country until May 10, 1939, when RCA—NBC broadcast a program from the New York World's Fair. A reviewer noted the "tremendous impact" of seeing and hearing an NBC announcer interview visitors to the fair. In 1984, the Library was given one of the earliest surviving television programs, a copy of an experimental broadcast made by NBC in 1939, entitled *Streets of New York*. While broadcasting continued on a limited basis, many technical and logistic problems remained to be solved. World War II halted most television broadcasting activity, but the postwar period saw an increase to one million sets in use in 1949 and to fifty million ten years later.

This phenomenal growth marked a new era in communications, one both applauded and condemned. In the early 1950s, writer Paddy Chayevsky characterized the small screen's potential as teeming with artistic promise: "Television is the marvelous medium of the ordinary. You can get in very deep with a very small moment. You can take an emotion too delicate for the stage or the movies

Presentation of kinescopes of the NBC-TV series *Wide, Wide World,* sponsored by General Motors, to the Library on March 11, 1956, was televised by a local news crew. When acquired, a Library official noted that the series—a precursor to the video news magazine—was accepted "so that future generations to come may see how Americans lived in 1956, what they did for amusement, and what they hoped for the future." Left to right: Davidson Taylor, an NBC executive; S. E. Skinner, General Motors vice president in charge of the accessory group; and Librarian of Congress L. Quincy Mumford. (*Photo by Mark English, Mark English Collection, Prints and Photographs Division*)

and shade this slight thing and let it grow." A decade later, some commentators bemoaned the banality of the product that had thus far been developed for the medium. In 1961, President Kennedy's newly appointed director of the Federal Communications Commission, Newton Minow, castigated members of the National Association of Broadcasters for having squandered television's potential, creating instead "a vast wasteland" inhabited predominantly with "game shows, violence, audience participation shows, formula comedies about totally unbelievable families, blood and thunder, mayhem, violence, sadism, murder, western badmen, western good men, private eyes, gangsters, more violence, and cartoons."

Television has affected many aspects of American life, from the way we get the news to the way we relax. Talk shows, such as Edward R. Murrow's *Person to Person* and Barbara Walters's specials, have brought worldly figures into living rooms across the nation for intimate conversations. Programs such as *Bonanza*, *The Cosby Show*, and *Seinfeld* have appealed to a diverse audience spanning differences in age, gender, and race. A casual site for shared culture, TV has brought war to our dinner tables—live and in color—lowered our collective attention span, and provided admirable and dubious role models for our children to emulate. Whether wonderland or wasteland, television's impact on American life and culture from the second half of the twentieth century on has been profound.

The Library's television collections include NBC's entire kinescope inventory—over eighteen thousand items from 1948 to 1970. Shows of interest in this collection include 18 episodes of the 1949 series of dramatized short stories *Your Show Time*, which featured the first program to win an Emmy, "The Necklace"; 35 programs from the documentary social history series of the 1950s and 1960s, *Project 20*, one of the few programs that Commissioner Minow singled out for praise; 354 programs of *Industry on Parade*, a weekly pictorial review of events in business and industry, produced from 1950 to 1958; 45 episodes of the pioneering dramatic anthology *Fireside Theatre*, including a 1955 program directed by John Ford; the 6 programs from the 1959 to 1961 series of specials *Our American Heritage*, starring distinguished actors such as Christopher Plummer, David Wayne, Judith Anderson, Burgess Meredith, and James Whitmore; 31 episodes of *Hollywood and the Stars*, a 1963 to 1964 look at the film industry, produced by David Wolper and narrated by Joseph Cotten; a

Howdy Doody was one of television's first stars. His NBC series entertained children from 1947 until 1960. The cast of the show included Bob Keeshan (later to become famous as Captain Kangaroo) as the first Clarabelle Hornblow, and Don Knotts as Tim Tremble. (*Moving Image Section*)

Sixties television shows often featured benign idiocy as a device to comment mildly on contemporary idiosyncracies. In this still from *The Beverly Hillbillies*, left, Buddy Ebsen as Jed Clampett, "a poor mountaineer," strikes oil and takes his family to live in modern Beverly Hills, where he meets his favorite moving picture actress, silent screen siren Gloria Swanson. Joe E. Ross, with Imogene Coca, discovers fire, or more accurately a match, in *It's About Time*, right. (*Moving Image Section*). (The Beverly Hillbillies, *Courtesy of CBS Broadcasting Inc.* It's About Time, *Metro-Goldwyn-Mayer*)

1968 visit to *Roberto Rossellini's Sicily*, with scenes of the island's history re-created by the renowned filmmaker; unedited Telstar coverage of the historic first live transatlantic satellite transmission of July 10, 1962; and the 1962 NBC News series *Breakthrough*, documenting the state of the medical field.

The popular NBC current events discussion show *American Forum of the Air*, which ran from 1949 to 1960, was known on Capitol Hill as the "unofficial Congress" because of the frequent appearances on the show of lawmakers seeking national exposure. Having begun as a radio show in the late 1920s, the program attained the distinction of being the only program to be transcribed each week in the *Congressional Record*. The Library's collections include kinescopes of over twenty *American Forum* television programs, sound recordings of television broadcasts of the show from 1949, and selected recordings of the earlier radio series.

Meet the Press began on the Mutual radio network in 1945, two years before its television debut on NBC. Having passed its fiftieth birthday in 1997, this acclaimed public affairs inquiry program is currently the longest-running series in television history. In addition to broadcasts of many of the shows, the Library's collections include manuscript materials donated by the show's producer and moderator, Lawrence E. Spivak. The shows display a half century of public figures being grilled each week by journalists intent on making news headlines.

As with *Meet the Press*, many successful radio series moved to television in the late 1940s and early 1950s, which provided a solid foundation for the new medium.

The Library's collections include variety shows, such as Ed Sullivan's *Toast of the Town*, situation comedies, such as *Amos 'n' Andy* and *The Jack Benny Program*; Westerns, such as *Gunsmoke* and *The Lone Ranger*; and historical programs, such as *You Are There* and *Cavalcade of America*, all of which began on radio. Television soon began to produce its own diverse set of original classic series, such as *I Love Lucy*, *East Side/West Side*, *Kukla, Fran, and Ollie*, *Camera Three*, *Lassie*, *The Danny Thomas Show*, *The Honeymooners*, *Playhouse 90*, *The Mickey Mouse Club*, *Naked City*, *Perry Mason*, *Leave It to Beaver*, *Twilight Zone*, *The Defenders*, *Alfred Hitchcock Presents*, *The Untouchables*, *Ben Casey*, *The Fugitive*, *The Andy Griffith Show*, *The Dick Van Dyke Show*, *The Smothers Brothers Comedy Hour*, *M*A*S*H*, and *Mary Hartman, Mary Hartman*, all of which are represented in the Library's holdings. The collections feature such eclectic highlights as 166 ninety-minute programs from the acclaimed anthology series *Omnibus*, including an adaptation of *King Lear*, staged by Peter Brook, with music by Virgil

The Honeymooners, one of the first situation comedies to be set in a working-class milieu, inspired subsequent hit series such as *All in the Family*, *Sanford and Son*, and *Roseanne*. In this scene from a 1960s CBS revival of the original, included as part of a 1966 *Jackie Gleason Show*, Gleason as Ralph Cramden ignites in characteristic anger as he tries to put out a fire, while his wife Alice (Sheila MacRae) looks on. Also seen are George O'Hanlon (with camera) and Madeleine Sherwood (obscured). *(Courtesy of CBS Broadcasting Inc.)*

The Bell Telephone Hour, which began on NBC Radio in 1940, celebrated its twenty-fifth anniversary show in 1965 with rebroadcasts of some of the stellar performances it presented since its first televised broadcast in 1959. Shown clockwise from the top are Maria Tallchief and Rudolf Nureyev, Joan Sutherland, Harry Belafonte, Maurice Chevalier, and Robert Preston. Nureyev and Sutherland made their American debuts on this show. *(Courtesy of Pacific Family Entertainment)*

Thompson, and starring Orson Welles; and selected dramas from *The Dick Powell Show*, including "330 Independence S.W.," directed by Sam Fuller. Unusual cult favorites in the collection include an episode of *The Hathaways*, a 1961 to 1962 situation comedy about a not-so-typical American family portrayed by Peggy Cass, Jack Weston, and the Marquis Chimps; an episode of the 1961–62 prime-time animated series *Calvin and the Colonel*, featuring the humorous travails of a conniving fox and slow-witted bear—characters based on the Kingfish and Andy from the controversial *Amos 'n' Andy* radio and television series—who were transposed into less-offensive animal garb by their creators, Freeman Gosden and Charles Correll; and a 1969 segment of the *Dean Martin Show*, featuring Dino with pals Orson Welles and Jack Gilford performing the song-and-dance number "Everybody Ought to Have a Maid," from the Stephen Sondheim musical, *A Funny Thing Happened on the Way to the Forum*.

Of historical interest are the thousands of hours of broadcast journalism covering the country's political and social life of the past half century. The Library's holdings include numerous television documentaries from the civil rights era, including NBC coverage of the 1963 March on Washington; "Walk in My Shoes," a program of interviews with African Americans from diverse economic strata, part of the acclaimed ABC *Bell and Howell Close-Up!* series; *CBS Reports: Segregation—Northern Style*, a 1964 examination of attitudes of white home owners in the North; *The American Revolution of '63*, an NBC three-hour news special; and *CBS Eyewitness* programs entitled "The Color Line on Campus" and "Breakthrough at Birmingham." A 1961 locally produced eighteen-part series entitled *The Complex Community* examined urban renewal and its consequences in Boston. Programs in the Edward R. Murrow—Fred W. Friendly distinguished CBS series *See It Now* include one on tensions between Egypt and Israel in 1956, a 1955 interview by Murrow with J. Robert Oppenheimer, and a 1953 examination of McCarthyism in the military. The Library holds much material on the Kennedy years, including ABC's *The Making of the President—1960*, written by Theodore White and based on his book, twenty-nine reels of CBS election night coverage from 1960, and 122 reels of NBC's coverage of the assassination of President Kennedy. In 1969, the Library was given kinescope prints from NBC of coverage of the assassinations of Martin Luther King and Robert Kennedy.

The Library's television holdings include many news programs dealing with the Vietnam War. As the fighting in Southeast Asia escalated in the 1960s, television played an increasingly important role in the national debate over the goals, rationale, and conduct of the war. Until the mid-1960s, television news

The MBRS collections of musical theater-related recordings, films, and broadcasts parallel the treasured special collections housed in the Library's Music Division. On March 28, 1954, all four television networks—NBC, CBS, ABC, and Dumont—broadcast *A Tribute to Rodgers and Hammerstein*, sponsored by General Foods, in honor of its twenty-fifth anniversary. The all-star cast pictured here performed numbers from the great songwriting collaborators' decade-long list of seminal musicals, including *Oklahoma!*, *Carousel*, *The King and I*, and *South Pacific*. The show was also noteworthy in that it was television's first million-dollar presentation. *(AP/World Wide Photos)*

tended to support unquestioningly the administration's viewpoint. Critical appraisals began appearing in national network broadcasts in 1966. The Library's collections include three influential programs in the series *CBS News Special Report*: "Fulbright: Advice and Dissent," a February 1966 interview with Sen. J. William Fulbright by Martin Agronsky and Eric Severeid, in which the chairman of the Senate Foreign Relations Committee expressed doubts about the 1964 Gulf of Tonkin resolution and the course that the war subsequently had taken; "Eric Severeid's Personal Report," from June 1966, in which Severeid offered his own pessimistic views after a journey to Vietnam; and the April 1967 "Morley Safer's Vietnam: A Personal Report," in which the correspondent presented a diverse range of impressions. The Library also has the February 27, 1968, *CBS News Special* "Who? What? When? Where? Why? A Report from Vietnam by Walter Cronkite," in which the respected anchorman for the first time expressed the view that the war might not be won, a telecast that deeply disturbed Lyndon Johnson, who announced one month later his intention not to run again for president.

Other items in the Library's collection of Vietnam-related film and television holdings include a short 1901 Lumière glimpse of a Saigon parade, *Fête de Fleurs*; eight *Nippon News* Japanese newsreels from 1940 to 1945; seventy-eight *Meet the Press* programs from 1961 to 1973, featuring guests representing the governments of the

United States and South Vietnam, as well as antiwar activists, such as Dr. Benjamin Spock and William Sloan Coffin, Jr.; sixty-eight programs in the 1966 to 1968 series *ABC Scope: The Vietnam War*, which some local affiliates refused to run; ten programs of NBC's *Vietnam Weekly Report* from 1966 to 1967; twenty-five CBS *60 Minutes* programs devoted to Vietnam, broadcast from 1969 to 1979; Peter Davis's hard-hitting documentaries *CBS Reports:* "The Selling of the Pentagon" (1971) and "Hearts and Minds" (1974); Frederick Wiseman's *Basic Training*, a 1971 study of draftees' training experiences; Emile de Antonio's 1968 antiwar documentary, *In the Year of the Pig*; the first American film made in Vietnam following the war's end, Robert Richter's 1978 *Vietnam: An American Journey*; and two thirteen-hour histories of the war, the 1980 Canadian production *Vietnam 1945–1975: The Ten Thousand Day War*, and the 1983 WGBH Boston/UK/French series *Vietnam: A Television History*.

After the South Vietnamese government fell in April 1975, the Library of Congress was given 527 reels of 16mm film that had been located in the embassy of the former Republic of Vietnam. These films, all of which had been produced in South Vietnam, include newsreels from the 1960s; short documentaries, including the series *Vietnam Documentary*, made in the 1950s; and propaganda films. The division has compiled an extensive finding aid to its Vietnam War moving image collections, one of many such aids included in the Library of Congress World Wide Web site.

Public Television

THE LIBRARY OF CONGRESS holds the nation's largest collection of public television material, much of it in master form. These programs document the development of noncommercial television, beginning with shows produced locally in the 1950s and proceeding to the present day. The collection features early production formats that eventually influenced commercial television, such as newsmagazines, miniseries, and various forms of children's programming. Holdings include productions of lasting interest for their sheer information or entertainment value. Most importantly, these productions document the latter part of the twentieth century in ways unique to this form of media.

Throughout its history, public television has been dedicated to serving local communities. Known originally as "educational television," it began not as a network, but as a group of individual stations throughout the country loosely united by common interests and purposes. These first noncommercial stations were licensed in late 1952, the same year that the Educational Television and Radio Center was established to store and distribute programs. As a service to these stations, a production arm was formed to create or contract for programs for distribution. This eventually became National Educational Television (NET).

The Public Broadcasting Act of 1967 brought substantial changes to educational television. Federal funds were appropriated for the first time, and many believed what had become to be called "public broadcasting" had broadened its mission. The Public Broadcasting Service (PBS) was created in 1969, still primarily to distribute, not produce, programs. After interconnection of stations was established in 1970, PBS did much to develop a national schedule. Today's public television audience is familiar with the PBS mixture of nationally promoted and uniformly scheduled programs interspersed with locally acquired and locally produced programs.

The Library received its first NET material—16mm prints of some five hundred and fifty titles—directly from the original distribution center in the mid-1960s. The programs, educational in nature, include the series *The Nature of Communism*, sixty half-hour lectures coproduced by Vanderbilt and Notre Dame Universities in 1964, and *Two Centuries of Symphony*, twenty programs teaching music appreciation, produced by WGBH, Boston, in 1960.

Much more material was received from PBS in the 1970s and 1980s, consisting of preprint elements for some ten thousand programs. These materials include such series as *The Basic Issues of Man*, twelve programs produced in the early 1960s by the Georgia Center for Continuing Education; and *Search for America*, a series on American institutions and problems produced by Washington University. The

A "TV Class" in a Rushville, Indiana, elementary school, circa 1952. Efforts to develop television for noncommercial uses date to the early 1950s. The Library is the leading national archive for public television broadcasts.

broadening interests of public broadcasting are also reflected in series, such as *Casals Master Class*; international acquisitions, such as *Civilisation*; and programs documenting the social revolution of the 1950s and 1960s, such as *Escape from the Cage* (on mental illness), *History of the Negro*, *Jazz Meets the Classics*, and *NET Journal*.

With the 1993 conclusion of a major agreement with PBS, remaining PBS holdings, including nearly eighty-five hundred master films and videotapes of NET material, have been donated to the Library. The Library continues to acquire a broad range of public television through PBS's gift of programs to which its distribution rights have expired. This is one of the largest of MBRS's television acquisitions—some thirty thousand master videotapes were available for transfer at the time of the agreement and will be preserved by the Library of Congress.

The Library also has collected public television programs through its other acquisitions activities, including copyright deposits beginning in the 1950s and off-air recordings from the late 1970s. These include some programs aired by public television stations but not necessarily distributed by PBS. Public television programs may also be found among the many smaller gifts that have come to the MBRS collections over the years. For example, the work of the National Public Affairs Center for Television (NPACT), which was created in 1971 from NET's Washington bureau, is represented in the WETA-TV Collection.

In the Wake of TV

RADIO AND MOTION PICTURES ON THE REBOUND

OPPOSITE. As television kept potential motion picture patrons at home, the movies sought to lure customers back by tempting them with features the small screen could not provide, such as 3-D, wide screens, and garish color, as in the climax to one of the final films that comedy team Dean Martin and Jerry Lewis made together, *Artists and Models* (1955). Pictured here with the duo, among other "models," are Dorothy Malone and Shirley MacLaine. (*Courtesy of Paramount Pictures*)

THE IMPACT OF TELEVISION radically transformed the radio and film industries. As radio shows and stars moved to television, much of the established network radio listening audience bought TVs and followed them. The remaining audience, however, was augmented by younger listeners who now tuned their car or transistor radios to their favorite disc jockey, or "dj," playing the latest hit songs. With more people staying at home evenings to watch network TV, the motion picture industry looked for ways to draw them back out, to give them visual excitement that they could not get on the tube.

While the postwar era saw the rise of the dj, a number of radio variety show hosts and commentators continued to be popular into the 1950s. *Arthur Godfrey Time*, one of America's favorite daytime radio programs, began as a local Washington, D.C., show. After Godfrey went national over CBS, *Newsweek* named him "the freshest voice on the generally stale 1947 network air." In 1970, the Library received broadcast transcriptions of Godfrey's enormously popular morning radio show from 1949 to 1957 as a gift from two of his writers, Charles Horine and Andrew Rooney. (The latter writer gained renown in his own right as a broadcast commentator when he joined the acclaimed CBS newsmagazine *60 Minutes* in 1978.) The collection of 3,000 recordings includes several rehearsals and warm-ups.

Commentator Raymond Swing established a preeminence on radio for his weekly broadcasts in the late 1930s and early 1940s from New York for the British Broadcasting Corporation and the Mutual Broadcasting System, programs that were held in great esteem by leaders in England as well as in America. Swing had open access to cabinet heads and was said to have taken ten hours to prepare each of his influential commentaries. In 1942, Swing broadcast for the NBC–Blue Network, and later for the Voice of America (VOA). As a protest against McCarthyism, he resigned from the VOA in the 1950s. From 1944 through 1964, Swing presented the Library of Congress with his papers, which include instantaneous recordings of several hundred broadcasts from his Mutual, NBC–Blue, and VOA programs.

By the late 1950s, although television had made deep inroads into capturing the national radio audience, network radio still produced a full schedule of day and evening programming, but with a different focus from before. NBC's vice-president in charge of radio, Matthew J. Culligan, cogently expressed this change in a 1958 talk when he stated, "Radio has become a companion to the individual instead of remaining a focal point of all family entertainment." This important cultural shift can be studied at the Library due to gifts by NBC and CBS of tapes containing complete network programming over extended periods of time. The NBC tapes

The materials pictured here belong to a file for a typical *Gang Busters* "case history" dramatized from fact, the broadcast of December 21, 1938, about bank robber and gunman George "Jiggs" Losteiner, convicted of murdering a patrolman. The *Gang Busters* materials held by the Library may be the most comprehensive American radio series documentation collection in existence. The "Colonel Schwarzkopf" portrayed in the script refers to the father, H. Norman Schwarzkopf, of the Desert Storm commander.

run from October 31 through November 7, 1955, while those from CBS cover May 13 through May 26, 1957, 7 A.M. to 11:05 P.M. At the time the latter gift was presented to the Library, Arthur Hull Hayes, President of CBS Radio, announced: "CBS Radio is proud to present this living record of network radio programming to the Library of Congress, where the nation's history is recorded for its scholars through both the written and spoken word." Tape recordings of broadcasts from CBS Radio's acclaimed actuality series of 1958 to 1959, *The Hidden Revolution*, which won the Peabody award, were also presented by CBS to the Library. CBS and the Mutual Broadcasting System provided radio coverage of the Nixon-Khrushchev

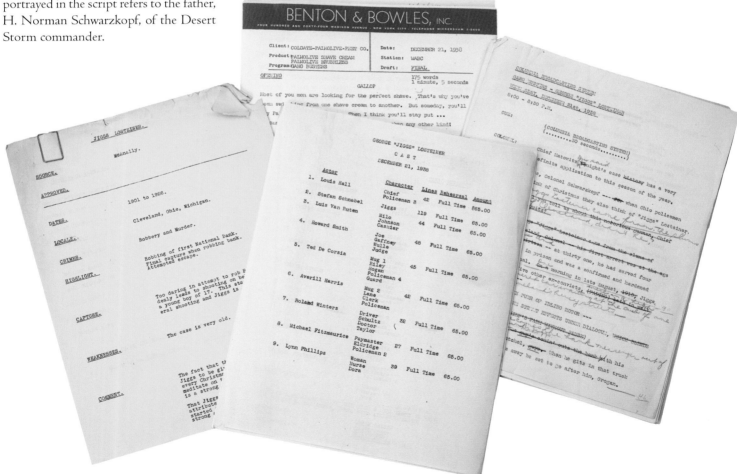

Science-fiction films flourished in low-budget 1950s thrillers, such as *Alligator People* (1959), from Twentieth Century—Fox's "B" lot. Beverly Garland reacts with some consternation after her husband, Bruce Bennett (at left), undergoes an adverse reaction to a serum produced in the Louisiana bayou. *(Twentieth Century—Fox)*

"kitchen debate" of July 1959, and the Library received a copy of the debate on newly developed videotape from Vice-President Nixon, to whom the Ampex Corporation had presented the gift. Radio broadcasting in the pivotal political year of 1960 can be heard as a result of a gift from CBS of 134 tapes, including coverage of the two political conventions. CBS continued to supply the Library with selected recordings of radio broadcasts through 1967, including coverage of the assassinations of President Kennedy and Robert Kennedy, UN Security Council meetings, and civil rights—related events.

In 1984, RKO-General Corporation donated the complete radio archives of the Mutual Broadcasting System's flagship station, New York's WOR-AM, comprising over fifteen thousand discs, the paper archives of the station, and materials relating to the radio career of writer-producer Phillips H. Lord, the creator of the popular series *Gang Busters* and *Counterspy*. The comprehensive collection includes

The Ron Korda Collection comprises every 45 rpm disc to reach the country music *Billboard* magazine Top Ten charts between 1958 and March 1996. The new prominence of women in country music coincided with the growth in popularity of the 45rpm disc during the 1950s. (When I Get Through With You, *Decca Records.* Child Support, *EMI America, Inc.* Are You Happy Baby?, *Capitol Records.* We've Come A Long Way, Baby, *MCA Records*)

copies of police files from which *Gang Busters* scripts were based, working drafts of scripts, production memoranda, and correspondence between Lord and the FBI.

The postwar years marked a period of sharp growth in the Library's National Film Collection. The 1942 decision to acquire motion pictures selectively through copyright deposit resulted in a booming increase in the quantity and diversity of films added to the collection since then. In recent years, some seven thousand to eight thousand titles have been selected annually. Films in the copyright collection represent all the major developments in American cinema since World War II, including film noir, the "social problem" film, Red Scare melodramas, Cold War science fiction and horror "message" movies, juvenile delinquency dramas, spy thrillers, sex satires, musical extravaganzas, epic Westerns, and religious epics. In addition to major American releases, this copyright selection has included independent films, short subjects, older films that have been rereleased, foreign films, educational films, industrials, commercials, newsreels, documentaries, animated films, and experimental cinema. Besides the films themselves, the Library's copyright collection contains an abundance of textual material that has been submitted by claimants for nearly all films copyrighted since 1912. This rich source of information includes a wide range of material such as scripts, dialogue continuities, synopses, shot lists, pressbooks, and other types of publicity material. For films considered "lost" (those for which prints have not been located in any archive or private collection), the collection of copyright textual materials can often provide crucial information for those studying twentieth-century American culture.

In the late 1960s, the Library began a cooperative effort with the newly created American Film Institute (AFI) to attempt to locate, acquire, and preserve some of our nation's thought-to-be-lost film heritage. This propitious collaboration resulted in the rediscovery of a myriad of supposedly lost films that reemerged in recent decades to the delight of fans and scholars, who are now better able to study and appreciate our distinguished motion picture heritage. Films recovered for public presentation in the first few years of the AFI-LC venture include Rex Ingram's *The Conquering Power*, with Rudolph Valentino, produced in 1921 just after the star's meteoric ascent to international romantic icon status; Gregory La Cava's 1926 comedy *So's Your Old Man*, one of comedian W. C. Fields's few surviving silent films; *The Vanishing American*, a tragic drama of Indian life, also released in 1926; King Vidor's 1928 Hollywood satire, *The Patsy*, with Marion Davies; and John Ford's 1930 drama *Men Without Women*, the first screenplay by Dudley Nichols and featuring an early appearance of "Duke" Morrison, later known as John Wayne.

barbara mandrell

child support

ARE YOU HAPPY BABY?
PRODUCED BY BRENT MAHER

DOTTIE WEST

B/W
RIGHT OR WRONG
PRODUCED BY
BRENT MAHER & RANDY GOODRUM
FROM THE LP "WILD WEST"
LT-1062

1392

LORETTA LYNN
We've Come A Long Way, Baby

MCA-40954
MCA RECORDS
MCA Records, Inc., 100 Universal City Plaza, Universal City, California — U.S.A. ©1978 MCA Records, Inc. ℗1978 MCA Records, Inc. — Printed in U.S.A.
WARNING: All rights reserved. Unauthorized duplication is a violation of applicable laws.

LORETTA LYNN
We've Come A Long Way, Baby

Hollywood reworked the classics of American literature for each new generation. In the 1960 *The Adventures of Huckleberry Finn*, exboxing champ Archie Moore sensitively recreated the role of the escaped slave Jim. Child star Eddie Hodges appeared as Huck. *(Warner Bros.)*

In 1969 and 1970, through AFI efforts, the Library acquired more than seven hundred features and nine hundred shorts produced by RKO in the 1930s and 1940s, over a hundred silent films donated by Paramount Pictures, the Maurice Zouary Collection of over 200,000 feet of historical films, including the 1920s De Forest Phonofilms described above, and the Hal Roach Collection of original negatives and master prints of over five hundred short comedies and thirty features produced between 1915 and 1942.

Also in 1969, the United Artists Corporation donated to the Library a collection of over three thousand films from the pre-1949 film library of Warner Brothers pictures, including 50 silent features, 750 sound features, 1,800 sound shorts, and 400 cartoons. In addition to Warner Brothers films, the collection includes over two hundred features made by Monogram Pictures Corporation, a low-budget "Poverty Row" independent producer specializing in crime and cowboy pictures of the 1930s through the 1950s, which gained new interest among young film buffs when French New Wave auteur Jean-Luc Godard dedicated his first feature to the nearly forgotten studio.

To the New Century

I N THE LAST THREE DECADES of the twentieth century, technological developments have continued to expand America's audiovisual frontiers. From the explosion in the home use of videotape to the introduction of the "information highway" into the homes of ordinary people, media has become even more intimately involved with the life and destiny of our country, as the range of links we now have to the wider world has expanded enormously. With the end of the first audiovisual century, the frontiers of preserving, maintaining, and in some cases restoring the ever-growing abundance of material that makes up our audiovisual heritage pose challenges for the library and preservation communities. The new century is marked by a number of significant legal and institutional developments that have fostered an enhancement of the role of the Library of Congress in audiovisual media collection and preservation. In this recent era, the Library's Motion Picture, Broadcasting, and Recorded Sound Division has stepped to the fore to provide leadership to meet these challenges.

The first law allowing copyright registration of sound recordings went into force in 1972. This act, which requires that all sound recordings published in the United States be deposited with the Copyright Office, has led to a sizable expansion in the Library's Recorded Sound Collection. The annual number of sound copyright deposits has risen from fewer than seventy-five hundred recordings in 1973 to almost nineteen thousand in 1994, making copyright deposits the largest source of the division's acquisitions. All kinds of music published in the United States are included in the Copyright Collection, as well as such unpublished radio broadcasts as those of the Metropolitan Opera and the New York Philharmonic.

In 1978, because of a change in the copyright law, it became possible to register musical works by submitting a sound recording rather than a musical score. People who could neither read nor write music could henceforth register their songs and music simply by making and depositing for copyright a cassette recording. This change in policy has fostered the preservation in the Recorded Sound Collection of political and social statements from American grassroots origins.

Copyright deposits represent a cross section of all kinds of sound recordings, not just music. Among the diverse materials that have been received and stored are self-help cassettes, language-instruction tapes, recorded books, recorded magazines, and cassettes on religious subjects. The collection includes autobiographical works by Elie Wiesel, Ed Koch, Sir John Gielgud, Joan Rivers, Hume Cronyn, Ronald and Nancy Reagan, Helen Hayes, Timothy Leary, Richard Nixon,

The Library's collections of film-related copyright deposit materials are extensive. This color and size guide to marketing Turner Entertainment—owned cartoon characters was included in a 1995 "Designer Droopy" merchandising packet. The original characters of "The Wolf," "Red Hot Riding Hood," and "Droopy" were all created by the legendary animator Fred "Tex" Avery for his frenetic cartoon shorts of the 1940s. (*Copyright © Turner Entertainment Co.*)

Sound recordings were not eligible for copyright until February 15, 1972. Later rewriting of the law, in effect since 1978, has enabled music to be copyrighted in the form of a sound recording, whereas before it had to be notated on paper. These two changes in U.S. law have resulted in hundreds of thousands of new audio acquisitions for the national collections. The *Color Photo Processing Cassette* shown here is "N-1," the first sound recording registered for copyright in the United States. The song, "You're All the Woman I'll Ever Need," on a 45 rpm disc, is the first musical composition registered as a sound recording.

Tip O'Neill, Lee Iacocca, and Maya Angelou. These works preserve not only the authors' words, but also their distinctive voices.

Although noncommercial radio predated the formation in 1926 of radio's first network, NBC, it did not become a major national force until after the inception of the first noncommercial network, National Public Radio (NPR), which began broadcasting on April 19, 1971, with coverage of Senate hearings on the Vietnam War. Funded in part by the Corporation for Public Broadcasting, which was created by the Public Broadcasting Act of 1967, NPR functions as a production and distribution center for news, public affairs, arts, and other cultural programs that are beamed via satellite to member stations throughout the country. NPR's popularity has grown steadily as the number of its member stations has increased and its shows have won prestigious radio awards, such as the Peabody and Dupont.

The Library's NPR Collection contains over twenty-five thousand tapes covering the network's arts programs from 1971 through 1991, including some that did not originate with the network. The collection contains many jazz programs, such as the popular *Jazz Alive* series, hosted by pianist Billy Taylor; Ben Sidran's *Sidran on Record*; and *Marian McPartland's Piano Jazz*. The collection also boasts of numerous broadcasts from the jazz festivals, such as those given in Montreux, Chicago, and Ann Arbor, music from many of the country's great folk festivals, including the American Folklife Festival, held every year in Washington on the Mall, radio dramas heard on such series as *Earplay* and *NPR Playhouse*, and classical music performances from shows such as *International Concert Hall* and *Composers Forum*.

In the most recent decades, the Library has made a concerted effort to strengthen its international motion picture and video holdings. Recent acquisitions include forty Cuban features from the Castro era; numerous Soviet features and shorts from the Stalinist era, including *Lieutenant Kije*, for which Serge Prokofiev wrote an original score; fifty-five Polish and Polish-American films in the Wladyslaw Waisman Collection; films made by members of India's New Wave directors; Egyptian documentaries; early Ingmar Bergman films, acquired from the Swedish Film Institute; classic Italian and Australian features; videos from Germany on reunification and the fall of the Berlin Wall; and Norwegian, Icelandic, Pakistani, Lebanese, and Israeli videos.

Recent years have seen a continuance of the discovery and preservation of rare and supposedly lost films from the cinema's earliest years. As an example of the international cooperation that has fostered these recovery efforts, the story of the

Dawson City discoveries is revealing. In the 1890s, at the far frontier of the Pacific Northwest in the Yukon wilderness, the town of Dawson City was becoming a center of gold rush activity. During the next twenty-five years, motion pictures for the entertainment of the populace reached Dawson City, the last stop after having been exhibited throughout the Northwest. Since the expense involved in shipping the films back to the owners was more than they were worth to them, they were stored in the basement of the local library. The reels of film eventually were used to fill in a swimming pool that was being converted into a skating rink. In 1978, these films were discovered during excavation work. Many of the cultural treasures found in that Dawson City swimming pool, including the only surviving film starring famed nineteenth-century actress Lillian Russell and an assumed-to-

Musical works registered for copyright are often topical, providing distinctive commentary on contemporary issues and events. These cassettes from the copyright collections were created during the Gulf War of 1991. The Library has received similarly vernacular recordings about the environment, civil rights, the women's movement, the Somalia operation, the Grenada and Panama invasions, and even the O. J. Simpson trial.

be lost early Harold Lloyd comedy, had been protected and preserved by the Yukon permafrost. Through the cooperation of the National Archives of Canada, the American Film Institute, and the Library of Congress, these surviving films were restored and copied to safety film, then added to the Library's collections of audiovisual wealth.

More recently, the Library acquired over a thousand American films previously held in the National Film and Sound Archives of Australia, which had insufficient storage space to retain them. This collection includes a number of silent films that had been presumed to be lost, including two Harold Lloyd

Serious, artful, and intellectually demanding films made for an international cosmopolitan market marked the height of postwar cinema. Ingmar Bergman's version of the Mozart opera *The Magic Flute* (1974), opposite, starred Ulric Cold and Birgit Nordin. Alain Resnais's *Stavisky* (1974), right, starred Jean-Paul Belmondo in a complexly structured historical thriller featuring a score by Stephen Sondheim. (The Magic Flute, *Sveriges Radio, 1975.* Stavisky, *Cerito Films, 1974*)

films, an early Broncho Billy Anderson Western, a 1924 feature starring a youthful Jean Arthur, and a Charley Chase Keystone Comedy.

During Richard Nixon's presidency, the White House acquired a collection of recordings selected by nationally renowned authorities with the intention of providing the White House with the best that were available in all genres of music, in addition to spoken word drama, prose, and poetry. The initiative, coordinated by the Recording Industry Association of America, was strongly supported by Mrs. Nixon. Duplicates of these 2,000 recordings were provided to the Library of Congress to form the White House Recording Collection. The collection was augmented during the Carter administration.

The preservation of our nation's radio and television heritage became national policy in October 1976 when Section 113 of Public Law 94—553, a section of the 1976 Copyright Law known as the American Television and Radio Archives Act, was passed. This act, which became effective in 1978, mandated the creation within the Library of Congress of the American Television and Radio Archives (ATRA) to preserve "television and radio programs which are the heritage of the people of the United States." Additionally, the law requires the Library to provide access to television and radio materials "to historians and scholars without encouraging or causing copyright infringement." Media scholar Erik Barnouw, who became the first Chief of the Library's newly created MBRS Division, announced that "a Rubicon has been crossed," alluding to a change in attitude on the part of institutions and the public at large with regard to recognizing the significance of electronic media in our lives and the need to collect and preserve it.

In the years since its inception, ATRA appropriations have funded the construction and maintenance of the MBRS video laboratory, authorized and funded the off-air taping of domestic television programming, and supported the acquisition and cataloging of such important television and radio collections as NBC, PBS, AFRTS, WOR, OWI, and NPR's arts and cultural programming shows. In radio, 5,000 BBC broadcasts dating back to the 1920s were purchased. ATRA holdings consist of approximately a hundred and fifty thousand television and six hundred thousand radio programs, making it the largest and most important broadcast archive in the United States.

The Library's Motion Picture, Broadcasting, and Recorded Sound Division was formed in 1978 in part to fulfill the mission of ATRA by consolidating the Library's broadcasting archival collections and programs into one unit. Motion picture and television collections, previously under the jurisdiction of the Prints and Photographs Division, along with recordings, formerly handled by the Music

OPPOSITE. The bulk of the Indian Film Collection of over two hundred films ranging from the silent era to the recent past was selected by a group of experts in Indian film, including the former Chief of MBRS, Erik Barnouw. The collection is particularly strong in films produced apart from the commercial mainstream, which have been acclaimed for their social and intellectual orientation. Filmmakers featured in this collection include the great Satyajit Ray (pictured here), Mrinal Sen, and Ritwak Ghatak. The collection was begun as the result of the passage of Public Law 480, which allowed countries dependent on U.S. aid to lessen their debt through payment with in-kind materials. (*Satyajit Ray, Calcutta, 1981. Photograph by Rosalind Solomon. Copyright © 1981 Rosalind Solomon*)

National Public Radio cultural programs held by the Library include the popular comic–automotive advice series, *Car Talk*, hosted by brothers Ray and Tom Magliozzi. (*Copyright © Richard Howard. Courtesy of National Public Radio*)

OPPOSITE. The extraordinarily comprehensive personal collection of one of the twentieth century's most popular comedians, Bob Hope, was donated to the Library in 1999. Included are scripts, photographs, radio and television programs, and Hope's personal, categorized joke file of over 250,000 jokes that he used in his monologues. Hope's files include this photograph of the Seven Foys' vaudeville act and the reconstruction for his 1955 film biography of Eddie Foy.

Division, became integrated under one umbrella. The division currently supervises all acquisitions of moving image and sound recordings, undertakes extensive cataloging activities to provide access to its collections, coordinates the Library's extensive moving image and sound recording storage and preservation functions, and operates two reading rooms for researchers. In addition to providing research materials and reference aids for countless scholars writing books and articles, the division has been the source for duplicated film footage and sound material for hundreds of television and theatrical documentaries.

With the great influx of material acquired by MBRS in recent years, the Library's audiovisual collections grew far more extensively than the ability of the division's staff to process them for use by researchers. Recognizing the increased importance of visual and aural culture for many scholars devoted to studying the past hundred years, Librarian of Congress James H. Billington has made public access to the Library's nonbook materials a priority of his tenure. As a result of his efforts, Congress has authorized considerable resources to bring formerly inaccessible sound and moving image materials under bibliographic control so that users can locate materials relevant to their research projects through cataloging and reference databases. In the past decade, hundreds of thousands of sound recordings, radio and television broadcasts, and motion pictures have been examined and cataloged for the first time. In addition, the Library's cataloging efforts have branched out into a number of innovative collaborations with other institutions and private collectors.

The goal of making materials in the Library's collections more widely accessible to the public has been furthered through the publication of items from the film and recorded sound collections in videocassette, compact disc, and audio cassette formats for mass distribution. Currently eighty-six folk recordings are available through retail outlets or the division's Public Services Office, in cooperation with the American Folklife Center. A range of classical music, including the historic series of Coolidge Auditorium concerts, has been produced on compact disc in collaboration with the Music Division. Recently MBRS has joined forces with the Smithsonian Institution in the release of a video series of films from the silent era gleaned from the Library's unique film collection. Additionally, the Public Services Office makes available congressional floor proceedings to senators and congressmen as well as to the public for noncommercial and nonpolitical purposes.

On May 10, 1983, the Library's Mary Pickford Theater was dedicated in a ceremony attended by the late Miss Pickford's husband, silent screen star Charles (Buddy) Rogers, and other such stellar personalities as Miss Pickford's stepson

Nitrate motion picture film is chemically unstable. As it ages, it begins to release acidic vapors which combine with the moisture trapped in the film emulsion to form nitric acid. This acid eventually begins to eat away at the image contained on the film (top photograph). Safety film, typically on a triacetate or polyester base, is much more stable (bottom). If multiple sources of the same film exist (as illustrated here), archivists can often successfully restore a film to its original state, by mixing and matching the best available copies.

Douglas Fairbanks, Jr., and two of her rivals in stardom, Lillian Gish and Blanche Sweet. In the succeeding years, the theater has functioned as a valued venue for filmgoers in the Washington area to appreciate select treasures in the Library's film collection in the manner they originally were intended to be experienced—as projections on a screen.

The public now has the opportunity to enjoy additional selections from the division's collections on exhibit in the new Bob Hope Gallery of American Entertainment. As a spotlight illuminating the great popular American entertainers of the past century, the gallery features highlights from such important division collections as the Gwen Verdon–Bob Fosse Collection, the Danny Kaye and Sylvia Fine Kaye Collection, and, of course, the Bob Hope Collection.

The Library of Congress is building the National Audio-Visual Conservation Center in Culpeper, Virginia, to ensure the permanency of the audiovisual heritage of the United States. The Center will provide a state-of-the-art temperature- and humidity-controlled archival environment for the Library's motion picture, television, radio, and sound recording collections, including separate vaults for the storage of nitrate-based motion pictures and two preservation laboratories, one dedicated to the preservation of motion picture materials and the other to magnetic and digital media. When completed in 2004 the Center will house all preservation and cataloging functions of the Motion Picture, Broadcasting, and Recorded Sound Division, with reference service for these collections remaining on Capitol Hill.

The Library has long been committed to preserving motion pictures, video, and sound recordings. The Motion Picture, Broadcasting, and Recorded Sound Division Magnetic Recording Laboratory has managed an audio preservation program for over fifty years. Motion picture preservation began in 1944, with experimental tests for copying the Paper Print Collection of early silent era movies. In 1948 the Library began a cooperative project with the Academy of Motion Picture Arts and Sciences to raise funds for restoration of the nearly three thousand films in the Paper Print Collection. When costs eventually exceeded the resources available to the Library and the Academy, Sen. Thomas H. Kuchel of California introduced two pieces of legislation in the U.S. Congress to fund completion of the entire project and to initiate preservation of the Library's nitrate films. That legislation became law in 1958 and began the annual appropriations that established the Library as the leading publicly funded institution dedicated to preserving America's diverse motion-picture heritage.

In 1970 the Library opened its own motion picture preservation laboratory. The laboratory is now a part of the Motion Picture, Broadcasting, and Recorded Sound

Gone With the Wind (1939)
—restored in 1988—

When blue or green dyes fade from a film it turns an odd magenta or reddish color. This condition, "dark fading," is common to Eastmancolor film stocks introduced around 1953 and often used for prints of earlier more stable Technicolor films. As can be seen here, keeping the original Technicolor negatives of *Gone with the Wind* in good condition allowed new prints to be made which restored the original colors recorded by the camera. (*Image courtesy of Warner Brothers and Turner Entertainment Company*)

Division's Motion Picture Conservation Center. It is presently located at the Wright-Patterson Air Force Base, near Dayton, Ohio, where motion picture vaults originally built to store armed forces films safeguard the bulk of the Library of Congress's nitrate motion-picture collection. Since 1970, the Center has preserved nearly twenty thousand feature films and short subjects produced during the period 1893 to 1951. The Center continues to operate full-time and is dedicated to conserving the approximately hundred fifty thousand reels of nitrate film in the Library's collection. The Motion Picture Conservation Center will be an integral component of the National Audio-Visual Conservation Center in Culpeper, Virginia.

Funding for the Library's preservation efforts for audiovisual materials comes from public and private sources. The major source is the annual Congressional appropriation, which is devoted to the ongoing effort to preserve collection items that begin to show signs of acute physical deterioration. Gift funds from a wide variety of grant-giving organizations, individuals, and other private sources are directed not only to saving deteriorating collections, but also to preserving movies, television broadcasts, and sound recordings of specific interest to donors

Maintaining functional equipment to play obsolete formats can be more difficult than maintaining the collections themselves. One paradox posed to preservation efforts is that materials in certain durable formats, such as the Library's two-inch open reel video tapes, must be transferred to new formats because replacement parts for the hardware necessary to play the original materials have become extremely difficult to obtain.

and the research community. Significant support for preservation projects is currently being provided by several major movie studios, which fund various essential staff positions in the Motion Picture Conservation Center. In 1988 the David and Lucile Packard Foundation provided a major grant to preserve the Library's collection of seventeen original camera negatives for films directed by Frank Capra. More recently, the chief source of private sector funding for audiovisual conservation by the Library has been the Packard Humanities Institute.

Preservation of the twentieth century's audiovisual riches is an immense task. Through cooperative efforts in the 1980s and 1990s, the archival and commercial sectors have come to the realization that collaboration is essential. The experience MBRS has gained in maintaining its huge audiovisual collections and in developing cooperative projects with other institutions, both public and private, to preserve those materials has encouraged the Library to take a leadership role within the preservation community. In 1988 Congress established the National Film Preservation Board of the Library of Congress. This group, representing all areas of the national film community of producers, film critics, educators, archivists, independent filmmakers, actors, writers, theater owners, and distributors, has become prominent in national efforts to coordinate and improve American film preservation. The Board and the Librarian of Congress laid the foundation for a national preservation program beginning with a thorough study of the current state of preservation efforts in the United States, including the commercial film industry and public and nonprofit archives. The Board's findings, published by the Library in *Redefining Film Preservation: A National Plan* (1994), included contributions from interested parties from all sectors of the American film community and outlined widely accepted recommendations for conserving America's surviving film heritage.

This Plan addresses in new ways thirty issues crucial to physical preservation, access, and funding for preservation. In it the film community advocates the creation of a public-private partnership in which funds raised to support preservation would be matched by federal money. In October 1996 this partnership became a reality when the Library and the U.S. Congress created the National Film Preservation Foundation.

The National Film Preservation Board also advises the Librarian of Congress on the selection of twenty-five aesthetically, culturally, and historically significant movies for addition to the National Film Registry. When a film is added to the Registry the Library of Congress is obligated to do all it can to ensure that it is preserved for posterity in its original format. Press coverage of the Registry entries has increased public awareness of the diversity of American cinema and the need to

For nearly fifty years, the Library's preferred preservation format for duplication of deteriorating audio recordings has been open-reel analog tape. Only recently has digital audio preservation become acceptable to archivists. The National Audio-Visual Conservation Center in Culpeper, Virginia, will include a Digital Repository for the storage and maintenance of the emerging format for preserved audio-digital files.

preserve motion pictures for posterity. In 1995 a national tour of Registry films was initiated to bring to Americans throughout the country, in small towns as well as in urban centers, the opportunity to see restored prints of American cinema classics.

Recognizing that America's recorded audio heritage faces similar challenges, Congress passed the National Recording Preservation Act in the fall of 2000 to set up for audio a preservation program that mirrors the successful National Film Preservation Board. This Recording Act creates a Preservation Board and Foundation dedicated to sound preservation. The law directs the Board and the Library to establish a Recording Registry, similar to that for film, to create standards for digital preservation, and to propose means for the legal dissemination of historic recordings for educational purposes.

The Library's commitment to sound preservation began at the end of World War II. The Recording Laboratory established in 1940 was soon expanded to create radio and other educational productions related to the war effort. After the war the facility was redirected to preserve those same materials. When the Library augmented its audio collections with Office of War Information and Marine Corps combat recordings, it took on the responsibility of preserving these recordings by reformatting them onto media more stable than those on which they were originally recorded. A full-fledged audio preservation program began in the 1950s with a Rockefeller Foundation grant to reformat field recordings in the Archive of American Folk-Song (now the Archive of Folk Culture). By

Publications created from the collections of the Motion Picture, Broadcasting, and Recorded Sound Division.

the end of the twentieth century the Recording Laboratory had preserved over a hundred fifty thousand hours of radio broadcasts, "live" music performances, poetry readings, oral histories, and field recordings.

Each of the four media—sound recordings, motion pictures, radio, and television recordings—began with an invention that captured sounds, images, or both, converted them to signals, transformed the signals into compact material forms or transmitted them through space, and converted them back to sounds and images for presentation in a different time and place. Although prolonged storage presents unique problems for each of these media, all four share the same need for conservation and preservation if they are to survive for later generations to experience.

With the "digital revolution," all four media may one day be preserved using the same technology. While digital formats may prove to be a lasting solution to the problem of preservation, the conservation of materials in their original formats remains a difficult, but crucial task for the Library. At the National Audio-Visual Conservation Center the Library will fulfill this mandate by storing digital and original analog materials at optimal preservation conditions. The Library recognizes its enormous responsibility to maintain audiovisual materials in usable condition for future generations. With a vision of the future and determination to confront the frontiers of preservation, the Library, at the beginning of a new audiovisual century, plans to prevail against the challenge to preserve for posterity the rich audiovisual heritage of our past.